ARE YOU MAD YET?

HOW ORDINARY PEOPLE CHANGE OUTCOMES WITHOUT BECOMING THE DAMAGE

2026 - USA EDITION

JUSTIN C. RYAN

Publisher: Soul Bridge Publishing, LLC, San Antonio, Texas, USA

Publisher Website: http://www.SoulBridgePublishing.com

Book Website: http://www.AreYouMadYet.com

About the Publisher: Soul Bridge Publishing is dedicted to books that connect the dots between core values, courage, vulnerability, shame, and spirituality. We seek works that help readers face hard truths with open hearts and translate inner transformation into real-world change, whether in religious, self-help, or political conversations.

Author: Justin C. Ryan

Author's Process: This book was researching, drafted, rewritten, and then placed in AI for final editing and content/organization refinement.

Edition: 2026 USA Edition (Rev. Code: 1.0.4)

```
ISBN: 978-1-971982-00-7 (paperback)
ISBN: 978-1-971982-01-4 (ebook)
ISBN: 978-1-971982-02-1 (audio)
LCCN: 2026903707 (Library of Congress)
```

Copyright © 2026 Soul Bridge Publishing, LLC

All rights reserved.

No part of this book may be reproduced in any form or by any electronic or mechanical means, including information storage and retrieval systems, without written permission from the author, except for the use of brief quotations in a book review.

DEDICATION

To my children, and to the generations who will carry our story forward,

I hope you never stop searching for what truly matters to you. Don't let the world decide that for you. When you find something worth standing for, stand tall, even if you're standing alone.

And never be afraid to speak what's in your heart. Your voice has power. It can help, heal, and change things, sometimes more than you'll ever realize.

Whatever path you walk, walk it with courage, kindness, and truth. That's what I've always hoped for you.

Your mother and I are beyond blessed and proud to have you each in our lives.
—Dad

CONTENTS

Introduction	vii
Prologue: Courage from Our Kids	xi
1. The Day it Looked Like Nothing	1
2. The Authoritarian Playbook	15
3. Seeing the Playbook in Action	38
4. How to Shape Anger to the Unique You	53
5. Applying Pressure Without Becoming the Damage	70
6. Choosing Your Lane and Your Risk	81
7. Holding the Line When Things Get Harder	89
8. What History Actually Shows Us About Change	98
9. If You're Still Here, You're Not Alone	105
10. What We Build	119
11. For the Children Who Are Watching	136
12. If You Do Nothing Else	148
Appendix A: Aligning Your Strengths With What You Can Do Right Now	153
Appendix B: High-Level Strategic Moves to Block Authoritarian Playbook Tactics	157
Appendix C: Go Deeper	163
About the Author	171

INTRODUCTION

During the Vietnam War, there was a man who went to the White House every night with a single candle. He stood there alone and stayed until the candle burned down completely. One evening, a reporter asked him what he thought he was accomplishing. Did he really believe that standing there with a candle was going to change the war or the administration behind it? The man answered calmly. He said he did not come to change them. He came so that they would *not change him.* That story (originally attributed to A.J. Muste) was shared by Glennon Doyle, and it stayed with me because it reframes resistance as something quieter and harder. Not performance. Not dominance. Integrity.

She also mentioned an essay by Michelle Alexander from 2018 called "We Are Not the Resistance." She wrote about how we are not the resistance in the way we have been taught to think about it. Justice, love, equality, and shared humanity are not new reactions to recent events. They are a river that has been flowing since the beginning of time. It cannot be stopped. It does not reverse course.

INTRODUCTION

The people and systems trying to roll it back are the ones resisting. *We are the river.*

If you imagine that river, you can imagine boats moving along with it. Not one boat. Many. Some are carrying immigrant justice. Some are carrying queer rights. Some are carrying racial justice, higher education, healthcare, peace, dignity. These boats already have captains. They have always had captains. Nobody needs to invent a new movement to matter. The work now is simpler and harder. Get in a boat. When you do, you are not the captain. You are a deckhand. You take direction. You do your part. And when you see the other boats, you do not shout at them for not being in yours. You shout encouragement. *Keep going. We are with you.*

And while we move, we do not become brittle or cruel. We do not turn movements into tests of worthiness. We organize and protest and protect, yes. But we also celebrate. We love each other well. We create spaces so alive and welcoming that people watching from the shore want to step in, not because they are shamed, but because they finally see somewhere safe to land. When they arrive, we do not punish them for what they did not know yesterday. We keep them. Because the point of staying in the river is not just to reach a destination. It is to remain human while we are carried forward.

This book is not a call to rage for the sake of noise. It is an invitation to notice what you have been quietly swallowing. The slow erosion of trust. The normalization of cruelty dressed up as policy. The way exhaustion has been weaponized so effectively that many good people now mistake numbness for peace. This book is written for those moments when you feel something is deeply off but cannot quite put language to it, when you sense the ground shifting beneath familiar stories about democracy, work, safety, and belonging. If you have felt confused, overwhelmed, or

INTRODUCTION

complicit simply by trying to survive, you are not broken. You are paying attention.

This is also not a manifesto telling you what to think or who to follow. It is a mirror and a map. A mirror to reflect how power actually moves in the modern world, and a map that shows where small, human choices still matter. You do not need to become an activist, abandon your life, or burn everything down to be part of what comes next. You only need to be honest about what you see and courageous enough to stop pretending it does not affect you. Anger, when grounded in clarity and care, is not the enemy. It is often the first sign that something in you still loves this world enough to want it to be better.

This book asks a simple but uncomfortable question and refuses to let it stay rhetorical. What happens when ordinary people finally recognize the patterns playing out in front of them, not as distant headlines but as forces shaping their own lives and futures? This book does not offer false reassurance or easy villains. It offers context, language, and restraint. It challenges you to sit with your anger long enough to understand what it is pointing toward, and to decide what kind of person you want to be when the pressure increases. Because the opposite of madness is not silence or compliance. It is awareness, shared responsibility, and the quiet decision to stop looking away.

Introduction References:

Alexander, M. (2018, September 21). *We are not the resistance*. New York Times.
https://www.nytimes.com/2018/09/21/opinion/sunday/resistance-kavanaugh-trump-protest.html

Doyle, G. (n.d.). *[Video about the river and the boats metaphor]* [Video]. Instagram. Retrieved February 1, 2026, from https://www.instagram.com/reels/DNtJzXs3A8d/

Erickson, D. (2017, August 14). *Holding the candle*. Erickson Media.
https://www.ericksonmedia.com/holding-the-candle/

INTRODUCTION

Muste, A. J. (n.d.). In *Goodreads*. Retrieved February 9, 2026, from https://www.goodreads.com/quotes/9340879

PROLOGUE: COURAGE FROM OUR KIDS

In January 2026, I was in my condo in Bangkok when my daughter's mother texted me.

She told me our daughter, a sophomore in high school, had decided to join a student-led protest and walk-out after third period. It wasn't something she had announced days in advance or debated endlessly at home. It was a decision she had made, and by the time I read the message, she was already on the road, marching with her classmates.

Around fifty to sixty students from her school participated. They joined similar walk-outs across San Antonio that day, part of a broader wave of high-school protests happening in cities around the country. The demonstrations made local news. So did the larger context surrounding them.

That same week, adult-led boycotts and protests were unfolding across the United States and in other parts of the world. In Italy, citizens protested the presence of US immigration personnel in their towns under the banner of Olympic "safety" preparations.

Different places. Different grievances. The same underlying signal. People were no longer content to watch quietly.

After reading the text from her mother, I messaged my daughter directly while she was on her march.

"I am so proud of you right now!"

I meant it without hesitation.

Later, I learned that during the walk-out, a driver in a truck had driven aggressively toward the group of students, forcing them to scatter. No one was hurt, but the message was unmistakable. Someone felt entitled to intimidate teenagers exercising their right to protest. Someone believed that anger, directed at the right target, might come without consequences.

That detail mattered.

Because it pointed to something deeper than a disagreement over policy. It suggested the beginning of a dangerous assumption taking hold. The idea that acting in the name of a political leader or movement might place someone above ordinary rules. That intimidation could be excused. That force, or the threat of it, might be justified if aimed at the "right" people.

This is not how a healthy democracy behaves.

I had known for some time that things were not normal. I had been paying attention. I had been reading, thinking, trying to understand what was shifting and why it felt different from previous political cycles. Knowing, however, is not the same as acting. Awareness can become a place to linger. A way to feel responsible without actually taking responsibility.

Watching my daughter step into the middle of that moment removed that distance.

She was not posturing. She was not seeking attention. She was responding to something she believed crossed a line. And she was willing to be seen doing it.

That clarity forced a question I could no longer set aside.

If a teenager is willing to accept risk to say that something is wrong, what does it mean for the adults who see the same thing and remain still?

This book does not begin with outrage. It begins with that question.

What we are witnessing now follows patterns that have appeared before in other places and other times. Patterns where truth is weakened, fear is normalized, and loyalty is slowly untethered from law. Patterns where ordinary people begin to test how far they can go, and whether the rules still apply.

We will talk about those patterns later.

For now, it is enough to say this. Knowing something is wrong is no longer sufficient. Awareness without direction becomes its own form of paralysis. And anger, when it arrives, is not a failure of character. It is a signal that responsibility is asking to move.

The question is not whether you are angry.

The question is what you are willing to do once knowing is no longer enough.

1

THE DAY IT LOOKED LIKE NOTHING

On the morning of January 30, 1933, a Monday, Germany was still a democracy.

The Weimar Republic's constitution was in effect. The parliament still met. Courts still operated. Newspapers still published freely. Political parties still campaigned, argued, and competed for votes. Citizens went to work, dropped their children at school, paid their taxes, and complained about the economy. There was nothing about that morning that would have told an ordinary German that the country they knew was about to end.

By afternoon, Adolf Hitler had been appointed chancellor.

He was not elected to the position. He was handed it through a back-room arrangement by conservative politicians who believed, with full confidence, that they could control him. Franz von Papen, the former chancellor, assured his colleagues that they had Hitler boxed in. The old guard would run the real government while Hitler served as a figurehead, a populist loudmouth useful for rallying voters but too inexperienced and too extreme to actually govern. "We have hired

CHAPTER 1

him," one of Papen's allies reportedly said. The conservative establishment saw Hitler as a tool. They were certain he could be managed.

That evening, Nazi stormtroopers marched through the streets of Berlin carrying torches. Thousands cheered from the sidewalks. Radio announcers, their voices no longer calm and objective but full of what one listener later described as "fanatic fervor," narrated the scene as though broadcasting a grand national celebration. Joseph Goebbels, who would soon become the minister of propaganda, wrote in his diary: "It is like a dream. The Wilhelmstrasse is ours."

Meanwhile, American newspapers treated the news with remarkable calm. The Cleveland Press ran the headline: "Hindenburg Names Hitler Chancellor after Compromise." The Philadelphia Evening Bulletin noted that Hitler "is not dictator of Germany and insofar his dream has not come true." From Washington, officials stated they regarded Hitler's rise "with complacence" and expressed faith that he would "act with moderation." The Seattle Times called him a "picturesque leader." In Paris, the mood was similar. One French newspaper assured its readers that there was no cause for alarm, since the new chancellor would "likely be more moderate than speeches have indicated."

No one panicked. Almost no one panicked. Because it did not look like the end of anything. It looked like politics.

Twenty-eight days later, the German parliament building burned. Hitler convinced the aging President Hindenburg to sign an emergency decree suspending civil liberties, freedom of the press, and due process. Twenty-three days after that, the parliament passed the Enabling Act, granting Hitler the legal authority to enact laws without legislative approval. Political opponents were arrested. Newspapers were shut down. Labor unions were dissolved. Within months, all political parties except the Nazi Party were banned. Within eighteen months, after Hindenburg's death, Hitler declared himself Fuhrer. The democracy was gone.

It did not collapse in a single dramatic moment. It was dismantled in a sequence of steps, each one building on the last, each one explained away by people who were either too invested, too frightened, or too hopeful to see the pattern for what it was.

Why This Story Opens This Book

The fall of the Weimar Republic is not obscure history. It is taught in schools. It appears in documentaries. Most people know, in general terms, what happened. And yet when you lay the timeline out plainly, one detail tends to surprise people more than any other: how ordinary it all seemed while it was happening. How many intelligent, educated, politically engaged citizens watched every step and still believed, until it was far too late, that the system would hold.

That is the core of what this book is about.

CHAPTER 1

Not Germany in the 1930s. Not one country or one leader. But the recurring pattern that runs beneath stories like this one, the pattern of how democracies lose their footing, and how the people living inside them consistently fail to recognize what is happening until the cost of recognition becomes unbearable.

The details change. The economic pressures are different. The cultural fault lines shift. The leaders wear different faces and speak different languages. But the structure holds with uncomfortable consistency: a democracy under stress, a population divided by fear and economic pain, institutions that bend instead of hold, a political establishment that believes it can manage what it cannot, a public that normalizes each new violation because the alternative is too frightening to face, and a narrowing window of time during which action would still matter.

If you have picked up this book, there is a reasonable chance you already feel something like what many Germans felt in 1932: a gathering unease that something in the machinery of your own civic life is not functioning the way it should. Not a single catastrophic failure, but a steady accumulation of moments that do not resolve. Language that shifts. Norms that bend without snapping back. Consequences that disappear. Institutions that hesitate when clarity is needed most.

You may also feel what many of those Germans felt: the persistent, nagging suspicion that you might be overreacting. That this is just politics. That someone, somewhere, has it handled.

This book exists because that suspicion, however understandable, has historically been one of the most dangerous forces in democratic life. Not malice. Not ignorance. But the quiet, reasonable belief that things will probably be fine.

You Are Not the Only One Feeling This

If you have had the sense recently that something fundamental has shifted, that political events no longer resolve themselves back into normal rhythms, or that the ground beneath everyday civic life feels less stable than it used to, you are not imagining it. That sensation is widely shared, and it is increasingly visible not only in conversations, but in measurable behavior.

For years, public anxiety has been dismissed as polarization, social media distortion, or generational overreaction. Each of those explanations contains a partial truth, but none of them fully explain what people are experiencing now. What we are seeing is not simply disagreement over policy or personality. It is a growing awareness that rules once assumed to be durable are being tested repeatedly, and that the mechanisms meant to correct abuse are responding more slowly and less predictably than before.

That realization tends to arrive quietly. Most people do not wake up one morning convinced that something is wrong. Instead, they notice a series of moments that feel off. Language changes. Behavior that once triggered consequences is reframed as strategic or justified. Institutions appear to hesitate when clarity is needed most. Each moment on its own is easy to rationalize. Together, they create pressure. That pressure is what many people are now carrying.

According to the Pew Research Center, a majority of Americans now report that democracy in the United States faces serious threats, with concern rising steadily across ideological, racial, and generational lines. Notably, this increase is not limited to people who identify as politically active. It includes large numbers of respondents who previously described themselves as disengaged or politically moderate. Gallup reports similar findings. Public confidence in Congress, the Supreme Court, the presidency, and the fairness of elections has declined sharply over the past decade, reaching levels not seen in modern polling history.

It is important to be precise here. Declining trust does not necessarily mean declining belief in democracy as a value. In many cases, it reflects the opposite. People tend to lose trust when they care deeply about something and feel it is being mishandled or endangered. Indifference produces apathy. Concern produces scrutiny. That distinction matters because it explains why declining trust has coincided with rising participation.

Engagement Is Rising, Not Collapsing

Contrary to the narrative that people are tuning out, multiple indicators show that many are tuning in more deliberately. Voter participation among young people increased substantially in recent election cycles, reversing long-standing trends of disengagement. Local elections, primaries, and ballot initiatives have seen higher turnout, particularly where voters believe institutional rules or rights are at stake.

Small-dollar political donations have also increased, especially to candidates and organizations focused on democracy protection, civil rights, and local governance. These donations are not driven by elite fundraising networks. They reflect widespread, decentralized participation. Labor organizing offers another window into this shift. The Bureau of Labor Statistics reports a resurgence of union activity across sectors that had seen little collective action for decades, including education, healthcare, logistics, and technology. While economic concerns remain central, many of these efforts explicitly link workplace conditions to broader questions of fairness, voice, and accountability.

Public protest activity further reinforces the pattern. Data from the Armed Conflict Location and Event Data Project shows that peaceful protest events in the United States have remained elevated since 2020 rather than returning to earlier baselines. These protests span a wide range of issues, but they share a common feature: participants increasingly frame their actions in terms of norms, rights, and democratic integrity, not just specific policy outcomes.

Globally, the picture is consistent. The Varieties of Democracy Institute reports that more people now live under governments experiencing democratic backsliding than at any point since the early 1990s, while resistance to that backsliding has also intensified. Freedom House documents similar trends, noting that civic mobilization often increases precisely when democratic norms begin to erode. These parallel movements tell us something important. Awareness and action often rise together.

Fear Is Rising Alongside Engagement

At the same time, fear has become more visible. People worry about professional consequences for speaking openly. Teachers report pressure and surveillance related to curriculum decisions. Election workers have resigned in significant numbers after facing harassment and threats. Journalists describe increased hostility toward basic fact-gathering. Parents hesitate before attending school board meetings. These are not isolated anecdotes. They form a pattern.

The U.S. Department of Justice has documented an increase in threats against election officials, educators, journalists, and public servants over the past several years. Even when violence does not occur, the presence of intimidation alters behavior. Researchers studying democratic erosion consistently note that selective threats can produce widespread chilling effects, particularly when accountability appears uncertain.

This is how normalization works. People begin to adapt not because they agree with what is happening, but because adapting feels safer than resisting alone. Over time, silence starts to look like prudence. Avoidance begins to resemble maturity. The cost of speaking appears to rise faster than the cost of staying quiet.

Go back to the story of Germany for a moment. In February 1933, just weeks after Hitler's appointment, newspapers were banned for criticizing the new government. Twenty papers belonging to the Catholic Centre Party were shut down in a single sweep. The Social Democrats saw their meetings broken up by uniformed thugs. And yet elections were still held on March 5. Voters still turned out. The machinery of democracy continued operating even as its substance was being hollowed from the inside. Many Germans told themselves that the system was working because the system still appeared to exist. By the time they understood the difference between the appearance of democracy and its actual function, the window for meaningful resistance had already closed.

This is the environment in which anger emerges.

Anger as a Rational Signal

Anger is often framed as something to suppress or distrust, especially in political contexts. But anger does not arise randomly. It appears when fear, concern, and moral dissonance reach a point where they can no longer be comfortably managed through explanation or delay.

For many people, anger surfaces after prolonged restraint. It follows months or years of watching lines move and rules bend without correction. It emerges when people realize that waiting for clarity has become a way of postponing responsibility. This is not the anger of impulsive reaction. It is the anger of accumulated awareness.

Importantly, this anger is not confined to any single demographic group. It appears among parents, veterans, faith leaders, civil servants, business owners, students, and retirees. It crosses ideological lines because it is responding to structural stress rather than partisan preference. The question is not whether this anger exists. The data confirm that it does. The question is whether it remains isolated or becomes coordinated.

Isolation Is the Real Danger

Authoritarian systems rely heavily on fragmentation. When people believe they are alone in their concern, they self-censor. When they believe their unease is unique or irrational, they disengage. Isolation turns pressure inward.

Evidence suggests that this isolation is beginning to break. Parents are forming networks to share information and coordinate responses to curriculum censorship. Faith groups are issuing joint statements defending pluralism. Veterans organizations are publicly affirming the rule of law. Professional associations are revisiting ethical codes that had long been taken for granted. Young people are often at the forefront of this shift. Student-led protests, walkouts, and organizing efforts are appearing earlier and with clearer framing than in previous generations.

This matters because democratic outcomes are shaped less by abstract beliefs than by collective behavior. When people recognize themselves in one another, coordination becomes possible. When they remain isolated, even large numbers can be neutralized.

CHAPTER 1

In Germany, the conservative politicians who handed Hitler the chancellorship were not fools. They were experienced, credentialed, and confident. What they lacked was not intelligence but imagination. They could not conceive that the system they understood so well could be turned against itself so quickly. They assumed that because the rules had always held, they always would. They assumed that because they personally did not intend to enable a dictatorship, one could not form around them. That failure of imagination, more than any single act of villainy, is what ended the Weimar Republic.

What This Book Sets Out to Do

Before going any further, it matters to be clear about what kind of book this is. Not because you need to be persuaded, but because moments like this tend to attract confusion, projection, and bad faith. When stakes rise, people try to simplify one another into categories that feel easier to dismiss. That instinct is understandable. It is also dangerous.

So here are the boundaries.

This is not a book trying to recruit you. It is trying to orient you. It is written for people living through a period where ordinary civic instincts are no longer sufficient, where the habits that worked in calmer times do not reliably protect what matters anymore, where waiting, trusting, and assuming correction may carry more risk than action. It does not ask you to abandon your life, your family, or your responsibilities. It asks you to understand the terrain you are moving through so you do not mistake passivity for prudence or escalation for courage.

This is not propaganda or party loyalty training. Propaganda simplifies the world so people stop thinking. This book asks you to think more carefully. Party loyalty training teaches people to defend positions reflexively. This book asks you to defend principles even when it is inconvenient.

This is a pattern recognition manual. Much of what feels chaotic right now is not new. It has happened before, in different countries, under different conditions, with different outcomes. The details change. The structure does not. Understanding how democratic erosion typically unfolds does not mean it will unfold exactly that way here. It means you are less likely to be surprised when familiar dynamics appear, and less likely to mistake early warning signs for isolated incidents.

This is a defense of democracy and human dignity. At its core, this book is about protecting the idea that no one is above the law, no one is beneath concern, and no group has a monopoly on belonging. Democracy is not only a set of procedures. It is a culture of restraint. It depends on shared norms that prevent power from becoming personal and disagreement from becoming existential.

This is not a call to violence or escalation. It takes nonviolence seriously, not as a moral ornament, but as a strategic necessity. Nonviolent movements succeed more often, last longer, and produce more stable outcomes than violent ones, particularly when broad participation is required. Restraint is not weakness. It is discipline.

This is a framework for action without dehumanization. One of the fastest ways movements fail is by adopting the very behaviors they claim to oppose. Dehumanization feels powerful in the moment. It also corrodes legitimacy, fractures coalitions, and justifies retaliation. You do not need to abandon your values to defend them.

And this is not moral superiority in disguise. It does not divide the world into the enlightened and the ignorant, the righteous and the irredeemable. It assumes that most people are capable of growth, reflection, and change, including people you may strongly disagree with. It does not guarantee agreement. It preserves the possibility of persuasion.

You do not need to be fearless, charismatic, or endlessly available to matter. You do not need to sacrifice your health, your family, or your future to prove commitment. Most durable change comes from ordinary people acting consistently, in ways aligned with who they are, over time. You have a role even if it is not dramatic. You have influence even if it is not visible.

THE LESSON OF JANUARY 30

The story of January 30, 1933, does not end with Hitler's appointment. It ends with the millions of people who looked at what was happening and told themselves a story that made it bearable: that the extremes would be moderated, that the institutions would hold, that the adults in the room had it under control. Those stories were not irrational. They were human. And they were catastrophically wrong.

The purpose of opening with that story is not to say that any particular country is Germany in 1933. History does not repeat that neatly. The purpose is to make visible the one pattern that appears in nearly every case of democratic collapse: the gap between what people could see and what they were willing to act on. The slow, reasonable, understandable process by which awareness is decoupled from response.

In the chapters ahead, we will examine how that process works in detail. We will look at the phases of authoritarian drift, the tactics that enable it, and the civic habits that either resist or accelerate it. We will look at anger and what to do with it. We will look at fear and how to function within it. We will look at what ordinary people have done in similar moments and what made the difference between those who held the line and those who let it move.

But before any of that, the first thing that matters is the simplest. You are not alone. You are not imagining the stakes. And the outcome is not predetermined.

The patterns producing this moment are well-documented. The responses to them are already underway. People are waking up. People are acting. And the future remains contingent on what happens next.

On the morning of January 30, 1933, Germany was still a democracy. By the end of that year, it was not. The people who could have stopped it were not stupid. They were not cowards. Many of them cared deeply about their country. What they were, above all, was *late*.

Chapter References:
ACLED. (2025). U.S. protest activity and political violence trends. Armed Conflict Location and Event Data Project. https://acleddata.com
Anne Frank House. (n.d.). Germany 1933: From democracy to dictatorship. https://www.annefrank.org/en/anne-frank/go-in-depth/germany-1933-democracy-dictatorship/
Bureau of Labor Statistics. (2025). Union membership annual report. U.S. Department of Labor. https://www.bls.gov
Facing History and Ourselves. (2016, August 2). January 30, 1933: The night of Hitler's triumph. https://www.facinghistory.org/resource-library/night-hitlers-triumph
Federal Election Commission. (2025). Campaign finance statistics. https://www.fec.gov
Freedom House. (2025). Freedom in the world 2025. https://freedomhouse.org
Gallup. (2025). Confidence in institutions. https://www.gallup.com
Goeschel, C. (2023). January 30, 1933, in the Nazi historical imaginary. Central European History, 56(1). Cambridge University Press. https://doi.org/10.1017/S0008938922001376
Hett, B. C. (2018). The death of democracy: Hitler's rise to power and the downfall of the Weimar Republic. Henry Holt and Co.
Kershaw, I. (1998). Hitler: 1889-1936 Hubris. W.W. Norton and Company.

CHAPTER 1

PBS American Experience. (2018, January 23). Nazis in the news: 1933. https://www.pbs.org/wgbh/americanexperience/features/fight-nazis-news-1933/

Pew Research Center. (2026). Public trust and democratic norms in the United States. https://www.pewresearch.org

Schleunes, K. A. (1970). The twisted road to Auschwitz: Nazi policy toward German Jews, 1933-39. University of Illinois Press.

U.S. Census Bureau. (2024). Voting and registration in the election of 2024. https://www.census.gov

U.S. Department of Justice. (2025). Threats to election workers and public officials. https://www.justice.gov

U.S. Holocaust Memorial Museum. (n.d.). Adolf Hitler and the Nazi rise to power, 1918-1933. Holocaust Encyclopedia. https://encyclopedia.ushmm.org/content/en/article/the-nazi-rise-to-power

U.S. Holocaust Memorial Museum. (n.d.). Hitler comes to power. Holocaust Encyclopedia. https://encyclopedia.ushmm.org/content/en/article/hitler-comes-to-power

U.S. Holocaust Memorial Museum. (n.d.). 1933: Key dates. Holocaust Encyclopedia. https://encyclopedia.ushmm.org/content/en/article/1933-key-dates

University of Kentucky. (n.d.). Hitler: Essential background information. College of Arts and Sciences. https://history.as.uky.edu/hitler-essential-background-information

University of Washington. (n.d.). Nazism in the 1933 Seattle Times. https://depts.washington.edu/depress/nazi_seattle_times.shtml

V-Dem Institute. (2025). Democracy report 2025: Autocratization and resistance. University of Gothenburg. https://www.v-dem.net

Wikipedia contributors. (2026). Adolf Hitler's rise to power. Wikipedia. https://en.wikipedia.org/wiki/Adolf_Hitler%27s_rise_to_power

Wikipedia contributors. (2026). March 1933 German federal election. Wikipedia. https://en.wikipedia.org/wiki/March_1933_German_federal_election

2

THE AUTHORITARIAN PLAYBOOK

A MAP, NOT A PROPHECY

This chapter is longer than the others. I need to say that up front because if you are someone who skims for the main point, this is the section of the book where slowing down matters. What we are looking at here does not reveal itself all at once. That is part of the design.

Most of us carry a mental image of how democracy dies. Tanks roll into the streets. The constitution gets suspended. Elections are canceled. People disappear in the night. It looks loud and unmistakable, a clean before-and-after moment when everyone suddenly realizes what has happened.

That is not how it works anymore.

In country after country, including nations that once considered themselves immune, democratic erosion has unfolded gradually through mechanisms that look legal, procedural, and even responsible on the surface. Courts are cited. Laws are passed. Elections continue. The language of democracy is preserved even as its substance thins. Nothing looks like a coup. Everything looks like policy.

That gap between appearance and reality is where doubt creeps in. You feel a tightening in your chest when you read the news. You notice that certain topics quietly disappear from mainstream discussion. You feel pressure to choose sides more aggressively, to stop asking certain questions, to lower expectations of institutions you once trusted. Meanwhile, daily life continues. Work. Children. Bills. Errands. No tanks. No announcement. No obvious signal that it is time to panic. So you start to wonder if you are over-reacting.

This chapter exists to interrupt that quiet self-doubt.

What follows is not a prophecy. It is not a declaration that collapse is inevitable or that resistance is futile. It is a pattern. Across different cultures, different ideologies, and different decades, researchers have documented recurring moves used by leaders who want to concentrate power and weaken checks on their authority. The details change from place to place, but the underlying structure is remarkably consistent: fear is heightened, institutions are bent, opponents are delegitimized, information is polluted, and over time people are taught to accept changes they would have rejected outright if those changes had arrived all at once.

The goal of this chapter is to give you a reliable map.

When you have a map, you can tell the difference between a detour and a dead end. You can notice when multiple warning signs appear together. You can stop arguing about whether each individual moment is "that bad" and start asking whether the overall direction makes sense. A map does not tell you exactly what will happen. It tells you where you are, what tends to come next, and where there is still room to turn.

This chapter is also meant to protect you from political gaslighting. Not the dramatic kind where someone stands over you insisting you are crazy. The subtle kind. The kind that sounds like "this is just politics" and "both sides do it" and "if it were serious, someone would have stopped it by now." The kind that makes each concerning development seem isolated, exaggerated, or your own fault for noticing. Pattern recognition cuts through that fog. It allows you to say, calmly and without hysteria, this is not random. This fits a known sequence. It gives you language that is steadier than outrage and more honest than denial.

One more thing before we begin. This playbook is not a checklist. Real countries do not move through these phases in neat order. Some tactics appear early, others never appear at all. Some moments that look alarming may fade. Others may escalate faster than anyone expects. And this is not a partisan weapon. Authoritarian tactics have been used by actors across different ideologies and party labels. If you read this chapter and only apply it to the people you already oppose, you have missed the point. The warning signs apply to behavior, not branding. Now we can begin.

How the Playbook Works as a System

When people sense that something is wrong politically, they look for a single decisive moment that proves it. A speech that goes too far. A law that obviously crosses a bright line. An incident so extreme it forces everyone to respond.

That moment almost never arrives.

What unfolds instead is a system of reinforcing actions. Each individual move can be defended in isolation. Each can be explained away as temporary, necessary, or no worse than what the other side did. It is the interaction between these moves, their accumulation over time, that produces lasting change. Authoritarianism does not function like a switch. It functions like pressure. Institutions bend before they break. Norms stretch before they snap. People adjust long before they openly rebel.

A permanent sense of crisis justifies expanded executive power. Expanded power is used to weaken courts and watchdogs. Weakened oversight allows corruption and patronage. Corruption binds elites to the leader. Bound elites help normalize abuses in media and culture. Normalization lowers public resistance, which makes further power grabs easier. At no point does anyone need to announce that democracy is over. The rules remain on paper. They are simply interpreted differently, enforced selectively, or ignored when inconvenient.

Modern authoritarians rarely begin by shredding the law. They work through it. Laws are passed. Courts are cited. Procedures are followed. For most people, this creates a powerful psychological barrier to concern. We are taught that legality and legitimacy go together. If something has passed through parliament or been upheld by a court, objecting to it can feel extreme. The playbook exploits this instinct by quietly changing the law itself, or by stretching old laws to cover new, more aggressive uses of power. By the time it becomes obvious that legal no longer automatically means just, some of the key guardrails have already weakened.

And then there is normalization. The first time a boundary is crossed, many people react. The second time, they argue. The third time, they shrug. What once seemed outrageous begins to feel like just how things are now. This process is accelerated by exhaustion. Modern life already demands constant attention. When political stress is layered on top of economic pressure, caregiving, health worries, and information overload, people naturally conserve energy. They pick their battles. They postpone engagement. They tell themselves someone else will handle this.

The playbook does not need everyone to approve. It needs enough people to disengage.

I am describing the system as three phases because it helps you see the shape. Phase One is about preparing the emotional and cultural ground. Phase Two is about capturing and tilting institutions. Phase Three is about consolidation and hard control. In real life, these overlap, stall, and sometimes run simultaneously. What matters is not perfect sequence but density. When multiple tactics appear together and reinforce one another, the system starts to tilt.

Phase One: Rise and Positioning

Phase One is where the emotional ground gets prepared. Leaders who want to concentrate power need the public to feel a certain way before they can start reshaping institutions. They need fear. They need loyalty rooted in identity rather than policy. They need opponents to feel like enemies rather than fellow citizens. And they need truth itself to feel unreliable. Phase One delivers all four.

Create a permanent crisis narrative. Almost every successful authoritarian project begins by convincing people that ordinary politics is no longer enough. This does not mean inventing problems from nothing. Real societies always have real challenges. Crime exists. Migration exists. Economic anxiety exists. The move is not to lie but to reframe these challenges as existential threats that cannot tolerate delay, nuance, or constraint. Politics is no longer presented as a process of managing disagreement. It is presented as a race against collapse.

The language shifts first. Words like emergency, invasion, chaos, takeover, and survival begin to dominate public discourse. Time is compressed. Every decision feels urgent. Every hesitation feels dangerous. When everything is framed as a crisis, restraint starts to look irresponsible.

This works because fear narrows attention. Under perceived threat, people naturally seek clarity, authority, and decisive action. They become less tolerant of ambiguity and less patient with procedure. That is not a moral failure. It is a human survival response. Leaders exploit it by keeping the sense of threat permanently activated. Problems are never resolved, only replaced. If one crisis fades, another takes its place. The system cannot return to calm, because calm would restore deliberation, and deliberation threatens concentrated power.

A permanent crisis creates psychological permission for extraordinary measures. Laws that would be unacceptable in normal times are reframed as necessary. Oversight is portrayed as obstruction. Opposition is portrayed as sabotage. Emergency powers that were granted with the expectation they would expire get extended again and again. Definitions of threat expand. New dangers are folded into old ones, so that what began as a limited response to a specific situation becomes a semi-permanent governing style. The public adapts to living in a heightened state of alert. Fear becomes the background condition of political life.

In early 1930s Germany, economic collapse and political violence were framed as evidence that the country itself was on the brink. The Reichstag fire justified sweeping emergency decrees that suspended civil liberties in the name of survival. In Hungary, migration waves were framed not as a policy challenge but as a civilizational threat, and emergency measures introduced as temporary became permanent features of governance. In the United States after September 11, emergency logics expanded rapidly, normalizing surveillance and security practices that reshaped expectations about state power for years. Different contexts, same mechanism: crisis resets norms.

If the permanent crisis narrative fails to take root, much of the rest of the playbook becomes harder to execute. Without amplified fear, extraordinary powers look excessive. Without a constant sense of emergency, institutional checks regain legitimacy. Without existential framing, political rivals remain opponents, not enemies. This is why movements that lean authoritarian invest so heavily in maintaining a sense of danger even when conditions improve. Calm is dangerous to them.

Exploit religion and identity. Once crisis has been established, the next move is to anchor that fear to identity. Politics stops being only about policies and starts becoming about belonging. Leaders do not create identities from scratch. They borrow from what already matters most to people: religion, ethnicity, language, region, national story. Then they position themselves as the only authentic defender of those identities.

The message starts subtle. We represent the real nation. We speak for the true believers. We protect what others want to erase. This framing turns political loyalty into moral obligation. Supporting the leader is no longer just a preference. It becomes a test of faith, heritage, or patriotism.

The critical shift comes when leaders stop merely representing an identity group and begin to claim ownership of it. At that point, to oppose the leader is framed as opposing the faith, the culture, or the nation itself. Religious symbols appear on campaign stages. Sacred language is woven into speeches. Critics are portrayed not as people with different views but as threats to our way of life. Journalists become enemies of the people. Courts are painted as hostile to tradition. The leader becomes the embodiment of the identity they claim to defend.

When identity and power fuse, moral reasoning shrinks. Actions are judged less by what they do and more by who does them. Behavior that would be condemned in an opponent is excused in an ally. People overlook corruption, cruelty, or broken promises because they feel that their side must be protected at any cost.

Over time, this creates permission structures. Harmful actions are rationalized as necessary for survival. Members of the identity group who do not fit the promoted version, or who interpret it differently, find their belonging questioned. This is not hypocrisy. It is moral triage. In a world framed as us-versus-them, defending the group feels more urgent than enforcing consistent principles.

Make opponents existential enemies. In a healthy democracy, political competition is adversarial but bounded. Parties clash. Power changes hands. Losing an election is painful but it is not the end of the world. The system assumes that today's loser can be tomorrow's winner and that everyone remains part of the same political community.

Authoritarian projects work to break that assumption. Opponents stop being rivals you argue with. They become dangers you must eliminate.

The shift begins in language. Opponents are no longer described as wrong or misguided. They are described as corrupt, criminal, or treacherous. They are enemies of the people, internal threats, foreign agents, or vermin. Their motives are assumed to be malicious by default. Once that framing takes hold, the rules of engagement change. If your opponent is just mistaken, you argue with them. If your opponent is a danger, you stop them.

This framing solves multiple problems at once. It simplifies complexity, because real problems usually have multiple causes and no quick fixes, but blaming a hated group offers emotional relief and a clear target. It redirects frustration, because when promised improvements fail to materialize, leaders can point to saboteurs instead of admitting their own failures. It delegitimizes accountability, because investigations and watchdog reports can be dismissed as enemy conspiracy. And it binds supporters together, because shared enemies create cohesion. Loyalty is tested not by competence or honesty but by hostility toward the right targets.

Existential enemy framing almost always slides into dehumanization. Opponents are compared to animals, diseases, parasites, or invaders. Their suffering becomes easier to ignore. Their rights feel less binding. Policies that would once have seemed cruel start to feel justified. Violence, when it appears, can be described as unfortunate but necessary. The moral threshold shifts without a formal announcement. In Nazi Germany, Jews and political opponents were steadily recast as internal enemies, laying the groundwork for escalating persecution. In Rwanda, Tutsi people were portrayed as cockroaches, making later mobilization for mass violence far more likely. Not every use of harsh rhetoric ends in atrocities, but the mechanism is shared.

Erode truth and attack independent media. If fear prepares the ground and identity binds loyalty, control over truth determines what can no longer be challenged. This step is not about banning information outright. In modern authoritarian systems, censorship is often inefficient and unnecessary. What matters is not silence. What matters is confusion. When people cannot agree on what is real, accountability collapses.

Independent media, academic research, professional journalism, courts, and regulatory bodies all serve a similar function. They create shared reference points. They allow people who disagree politically to still argue within a common reality. You do not need to convince everyone that your version of events is correct. You only need to convince enough people that no version can be trusted. Once truth feels subjective, power fills the vacuum.

The erosion follows a predictable escalation. It starts with legitimate criticism, because media does make mistakes and journalists do have biases. The playbook exploits this by turning critique into total delegitimization. They are biased becomes they are corrupt becomes they are controlled becomes they are enemies. Independent outlets are no longer flawed participants in public life. They are hostile actors. Corrections are framed as cover-ups. Investigations are dismissed as sabotage. Audiences are trained not to evaluate evidence but to dismiss sources reflexively.

Parallel information ecosystems are built. Friendly outlets are promoted. Dissenting voices are drowned out, mocked, or harassed. Algorithms amplify outrage and affirmation. Within these ecosystems, repetition matters more than accuracy. Emotional resonance matters more than verification. Narratives become self-sealing. Contradictory evidence is interpreted as further proof of conspiracy.

Lies can be disproven. Confusion cannot. When people believe that truth is unknowable, they disengage. When they disengage, those in power face less resistance. People stop asking what is true and start asking what is safe to say.

Divide and conquer society. A society that can coordinate is difficult to dominate. A society that is fragmented, suspicious, and internally hostile can be controlled with far less force. This is why authoritarian movements do not merely tolerate polarization. They cultivate it. Division is not a failure of leadership. It is a strategy.

The move takes existing differences and hardens them. Political disagreement becomes cultural identity. Cultural identity becomes moral hierarchy. Moral hierarchy becomes justification for exclusion. Instead of many disagreements coexisting, society is reorganized around a single consuming conflict. Every issue is pulled into it. Every institution is pressured to take sides. Neutrality becomes suspect.

Leaders amplify culture war issues that trigger strong emotional responses, often ones with limited relevance to daily governance but high symbolic value. Media ecosystems reward outrage. Social platforms promote content that provokes anger and fear. Over time, people are trained to see one another not as neighbors with differing views but as representatives of hostile camps. You are encouraged to laugh at the other side's pain. You are told compromise is weakness. You are warned that cooperation equals betrayal.

Polarization fractures potential coalitions. People who might otherwise unite around shared concerns like corruption or economic fairness are kept apart by cultural hostility. It exhausts the public so that people become reactive rather than strategic. It obscures accountability because when everything is framed as a battle between sides, failures can always be blamed on the enemy. And a divided society polices itself. Social punishment replaces legal punishment. Fear of ostracism replaces fear of arrest. People internalize limits without being told. That is efficient power.

Use democratic language to hollow out democracy. The final move of Phase One is perhaps the most disorienting. Leaders do not abandon the language of democracy. They flood it. Referendums are called, but only on questions the government has already decided. Public consultations are held, but results are ignored or selectively cited. Opponents are called anti-democratic for resisting measures that were passed through democratic procedures, even when those procedures have been distorted.

This creates a powerful rhetorical trap. If a leader holds a referendum and uses the result to consolidate power, anyone who objects can be portrayed as anti-democratic. The word democracy is turned into armor for the very people dismantling it.

By the end of Phase One, most people still believe they are living in a democracy. Elections exist. Institutions exist. Rights exist on paper. What has changed is expectation. People no longer expect institutions to constrain power consistently. They no longer expect rules to apply equally. They no longer expect truth to settle disputes. Phase One does not collapse democracy. It conditions society to accept its hollowing.

What Phase One Feels Like From Where You Sit

Let me step out of the framework for a moment and talk about what this actually feels like when you are living through it.

You notice that political conversations are more tense. Humor disappears from certain topics. News coverage feels breathless and repetitive, always cycling back to the same threat. You feel pressure to pick a side, to stop asking questions that once felt reasonable. Your daily life may look largely unchanged. That mismatch between rhetoric and reality is disorienting.

You notice fatigue. Permanent crisis is exhausting. You swing between vigilance and numbness. Both responses make it harder to think clearly. You start to disengage because it feels emotionally healthier to tune out than to live in constant alarm. That disengagement is exactly what the crisis narrative is designed to produce.

Family conversations become strained. Friendships bend. Workplaces grow cautious. You learn which topics to avoid. You start self-censoring, not because you changed your mind but because the cost of speaking feels higher than the cost of silence. You feel isolated even among people who share your values.

You find yourself unsure which sources to trust. You notice friends dismissing credible reporting without reading it. You feel exhausted by fact-checking, or tempted to stop trying altogether. You begin to question your own judgment.

And through all of this, no one has declared martial law. No tanks have appeared. Elections are still happening. The gap between what you feel and what you can prove makes you wonder whether you are the problem.

You are not the problem. That feeling of disorientation is a feature of the system, not a bug in your perception.

Phase Two: Capture and Tilt of Institutions

Phase One is about shaping how people feel and talk. Phase Two is about rewiring the machinery that decides who has power, how decisions are made, and who can stop them.

This is when things get serious without looking dramatic. The moves of Phase Two are usually technical, spread out over time, and explained in dense language about efficiency, modernization, or security. A new rule here. A restructuring there. A change in jurisdiction somewhere else. Each step can be defended in isolation. Few are large enough by themselves to feel like an emergency. It is only when you see them together that the pattern becomes clear: power is flowing steadily toward the executive, and the institutions that might resist are being bent or weakened.

Resistance also becomes costlier. In Phase One, pushing back meant arguing about narratives, calling out lies, defending targeted groups. Difficult, but relatively low risk. In Phase Two, speaking out may mean confronting superiors in the civil service, challenging judges who now owe their seats to the ruling party, or criticizing reforms that have been sold to the public as patriotic. Journalists and activists may find themselves facing legal harassment rather than just angry comments.

Phase Two moves on five fronts simultaneously.

Expand executive power. At the center of Phase Two is a simple project: expand what the executive can do and shrink the ability of anyone else to say no. Laws are amended to give presidents or prime ministers new decree powers. Procedures are changed so that certain decisions no longer require full debate. Oversight requirements are relaxed. Constitutional clauses meant for rare emergencies are reinterpreted to cover a much wider range of situations. On their own, each change can be defended as cutting red tape or responding to crisis. Over time, they add up to an executive who can act with far fewer constraints. Emergency powers are the favorite tool. They are granted as temporary, extended as necessary, and eventually become permanent.

Undermine courts and the rule of law. If expanding executive power is about what leaders can do, undermining courts is about shrinking who can stop them. The goal is rarely to abolish courts outright. It is to transform them from referees into reliable team players. Appointment rules are changed so the governing party controls who becomes a judge. The size of key courts is altered so new, loyal judges can be added quickly. Retirement ages are adjusted to force out inconvenient judges. Disciplinary bodies are created that can punish judges on vague grounds like undermining the dignity of the judiciary, signaling to everyone else that ruling against the government has personal consequences. Meanwhile, leaders publicly attack any court that issues an unfavorable ruling, portraying judges as unelected elites blocking the will of the people. Judges self-censor before cases ever reach decision.

Rig the electoral playing field while keeping the rituals of voting. Elections continue, which is precisely the point. The existence of elections creates the appearance of legitimacy. The task is not to eliminate voting but to tilt every aspect of the process so heavily that outcomes are effectively predetermined. Voter registration rules are changed to suppress turnout in opposition areas. Districts are drawn to dilute opposing votes. State media provides favorable coverage of the government and hostile coverage of challengers. Opposition candidates face tax audits, legal investigations, or bureaucratic obstacles. Campaign finance laws are selectively enforced. Independent election observers are restricted, discredited, or replaced. The election still happens. It just no longer functions as an actual contest.

Co-opt or cripple independent watchdogs. Even when courts and elections are weakened, democracies have other institutions designed to keep power honest: auditors, inspectors general, anti-corruption commissions, ethics boards, central banks. For a leadership that wants fewer constraints, these bodies are dangerous if they work as intended. The aim is to neutralize them without the optics of abolishing them. Key oversight posts are filled with loyalists. Legal mandates are revised to narrow what these bodies can investigate. Budgets are trimmed. Investigative teams are left understaffed. Agencies are reorganized in ways that disrupt ongoing work. None of this looks like an attack on oversight. Each step is framed as cost-saving or streamlining. But the cumulative effect is that the institutions meant to guard the public interest have less time, fewer tools, and weaker independence. High-profile investigations start targeting opposition figures while allies of the regime never face scrutiny. The law has not disappeared. It has become a weapon used unevenly.

Personalize power and buy elites. As institutions bend and watchdogs weaken, power stops flowing through offices and rules and starts flowing through personal relationships. Officials answer to the leader rather than to the law. Careers, contracts, and legal safety depend less on merit and more on loyalty. Senior posts in the civil service, security agencies, and state enterprises are reserved for people whose main qualification is personal reliability. Business leaders learn that access to contracts and regulatory leniency depends on staying in the regime's good graces. Those who resist find themselves audited, prosecuted, or frozen out.

Corruption becomes glue. Elites benefit from lucrative deals and insider opportunities, but those same benefits make them vulnerable. The more questionable the arrangement, the more they stand to lose if a genuinely independent government comes to power. Even those who privately dislike the regime feel they cannot risk real change.

Taken together, these five fronts produce what scholars call democratic erosion or hybrid regimes: systems that still hold elections and cite constitutions but where real competition and accountability are steadily reduced. Citizens can still vote, but it matters less. Courts still exist, but they are more cautious. Oversight bodies still operate, but mostly on paper. The architecture remains. The building functions very differently.

For ordinary citizens, Phase Two looks like a blur of legal jargon and political argument. You hear that a state of emergency has been declared or that a new decree power has been granted without feeling an immediate effect in your daily life. It is easy to assume that lawyers and judges will keep everything in bounds. The risk is that by the time it becomes clear how far those bounds have moved, much of the old constraint has already been given away.

Phase Three: Consolidation and Hard Control

If Phase One prepares the ground and Phase Two rewires the machinery, Phase Three is what happens when both succeed and no one stops them.

This is the phase that most people picture when they think of authoritarianism, but by the time it arrives, it often looks quieter than you would expect. There may be no large-scale civil war, no daily images of tanks and barricades. People go to work, attend school, watch sports, scroll their phones. Tourists visit and see a country that appears orderly and even prosperous. The loudest shocks have already happened. What remains is a heavy stillness.

That quiet is misleading. It does not mean consent. It means that key institutions have been brought into alignment, that open resistance carries high personal cost, and that enough people have decided that survival requires keeping their heads down. Fear, confusion, and adapted expectations do the work that open violence once did.

Monopolize force and apply it selectively. The regime tightens control over the security sector. Leadership positions are filled with loyal officers. Chains of command are centralized. Parallel units are created, interior ministry forces, presidential guards, intelligence branches, whose loyalties run directly to the regime rather than the constitution. In some cases, semi-official militias are armed or tolerated, giving the regime deniability for certain abuses while signaling its reach.

Modern authoritarian regimes that grew out of formal democracies tend to rely on selective rather than mass repression. Instead of rounding up huge populations indiscriminately, they focus on individuals and groups who are organizers, catalysts, or symbols: opposition leaders, journalists, activists, lawyers, student leaders, local notables. The message is that certain lines will be punished, even if everyday grumbling is tolerated.

Selective repression does two things at once. It removes key nodes of resistance by decapitating leadership. And it sends a signal to everyone else. When people see that someone like them has been arrested, harassed, disappeared, or ruined, they adjust their own behavior. The regime does not need to punish everyone. It needs to punish enough people, in visible enough ways, that the rest decide it is not worth the risk. Chile under Pinochet used brutal, publicized repression in the early years to create a climate of fear that lasted long after the worst violence subsided. More recent regimes in Egypt and Belarus have combined high-profile crackdowns with ongoing background harassment to keep civil society fragmented and cautious.

Weaponize fear into a punitive culture. Once the state has the capacity to punish selectively, the next move is to make fear do as much of the work as possible. The goal is not only that people fear the government but that they begin to fear one another: neighbors, coworkers, even family members who might report them, shame them, or turn away when they are targeted.

Leaders and aligned media normalize harsh language about opponents. Harassment and threats are excused, minimized, or celebrated. Online mobs are allowed, sometimes quietly encouraged, to go after those who step out of line. Everyday citizens learn that joining the pile-on is safer than defending someone who has been singled out.

Rules remain vague. People are never entirely sure where the line is, only that it moves and that crossing it can be costly. That uncertainty makes fear more powerful because it causes people to overcorrect. They censor themselves more than the law strictly requires. Over time, citizens internalize the idea that missteps must be punished, that mercy is weakness, and that those who attract negative attention probably brought it on themselves. The target is isolated twice. First by the state. Then by the community.

Deploy digital authoritarianism. In earlier eras, regimes relied on physical surveillance, informants, and control of print and broadcast media. Now they add a digital layer. The aim is to shape the entire online environment so that dissent is harder to organize, truth is harder to find, and loyalty feels like the path of least resistance. Social media platforms are banned or periodically shut down during protests. Surveillance tools monitor private communications. Algorithms are manipulated to promote government-friendly content. Activists are targeted with sophisticated spyware. The space for genuine criticism is technically allowed but practically drowned out, while the space for noise and loyal messaging is enlarged.

Rewrite history and control education. The final tool of consolidation is the longest game. History textbooks are revised so that episodes of resistance, democratic struggle, or successful opposition movements are downplayed, reframed, or omitted. Children grow up with a version of history in which authoritarian rule appears as a natural continuation of national destiny. Civic education is reshaped to emphasize loyalty and obedience rather than rights and critical thinking. University autonomy is curtailed. Sensitive research topics become risky. Cultural institutions are steered toward celebrating the regime and marginalizing works that challenge it. Each change is small enough to justify on its own, correcting past bias, strengthening national pride, stopping the politicization of education. The cumulative effect is profound. When an entire generation is taught that dissenters are villains and the current order is the natural endpoint of history, the imaginative space for genuine change shrinks.

Reversing consolidation is possible, but it demands more than individual courage or better arguments. The system has been designed to isolate opponents, punish leaders, and fragment society so that no single group can force change alone. That is why successful transitions away from entrenched authoritarian rule almost always involve mass action and broad coalitions: large numbers of people acting together in ways that alter the calculations of those who hold power. This does not mean everyone must agree on everything. It means enough people, across enough sectors, decide that the existing arrangement is no longer tolerable and that they are willing to take coordinated risks to reshape it.

Why Good People Miss This While It Is Happening

CHAPTER 2

If you have ever looked back at a country's slide into authoritarianism and wondered how people let this happen, this section is for you. The point is not to scold anyone. It is to understand why decent, thoughtful people so often recognize the pattern late, and why that delay is human rather than proof of cowardice.

The first reason is simple: life keeps going. Even as rhetoric hardens and institutions are bent, most people are still trying to hold down jobs, care for family, manage health, and pay bills. Politics is not their full-time occupation. When warning signs appear, they land alongside a thousand other demands on attention. It is easier, and often feels more responsible, to assume that someone else will handle the big problems.

The second reason is fatigue. There are constant scandals, outrages, and controversies. Every week brings something that could justify a march or a petition. No one can respond to everything. People pick their battles. They tune out for stretches to protect their mental health. They tell themselves they will re-engage when it is really serious, without realizing that seriousness is measured not by one dramatic moment but by the accumulation of many smaller ones.

Then there is legality bias. If something has passed through formal channels, it cannot be that bad. We trust that laws and courts are designed to prevent the worst from happening. Authoritarian projects exploit this by working through legal mechanisms wherever possible: passing laws, following procedures, citing constitutional clauses. The result is that people hesitate to describe what they see as erosion because doing so seems like accusing the entire legal order of failure.

Identity pressure adds another layer. When politics is tied to religion, nationality, or party, speaking out can feel like betraying your own. People who see problems may fear being labeled disloyal, unpatriotic, or elitist. It is often easier to stay quiet or rationalize that your side is still better than the alternative, even when your side is crossing lines you would once have considered unacceptable.

And finally, there is uncertainty itself. Authoritarian playbooks are designed to produce ambiguity: a mix of real problems and manufactured ones, real reforms and power grabs, real threats and exaggerated ones. People who are cautious by nature do not want to overreact. Many wait for a level of clarity that never arrives, a moment when everyone agrees that now it is definitely authoritarian. That moment rarely comes.

If you recognize yourself in any of this, the point is not to feel guilty. Shame is a poor fuel for sustained action. Missing the pattern for a while does not make you uniquely flawed. It makes you normal. Authoritarian systems are built to exploit normal human tendencies: to trust legal forms, to prioritize daily life, to avoid conflict with our own communities, to conserve emotional energy. Restoring your own dignity here means allowing yourself to say, of course I wanted to believe things would work out. Of course I hesitated. Of course I was tired. From that place, it becomes easier to ask a different question. Not why did I not see this sooner, but now that I see more clearly, what can I do with the time and influence I have?

How to Use This Chapter Going Forward

You do not need to memorize this chapter. Trying to hold every phase and tactic in your head at once is a recipe for overload. Instead, think of this as a reference map you can return to when something you see or feel does not sit right. When a headline, a new law, or a shift in tone makes you uneasy, come back here and ask: does this resemble any of these moves? Is it an isolated event, or does it reinforce a pattern I am starting to recognize?

CHAPTER 2

The chapters that follow build on this map in three ways.

First, they will talk about anger, how to honor it without letting it burn you out or turn you into a mirror of the thing you are resisting. Understanding the playbook gives your anger context. Instead of reacting to the latest outrage, you can see where that outrage fits in the larger sequence. That makes it easier to distinguish between news-cycle drama and deeper structural changes, and to decide where your limited energy is best spent.

Second, they will introduce the idea of covenant, the underlying agreements that make shared life possible: that losers of elections accept the result, that institutions are more than tools, that opponents remain part of the same community. This chapter showed how those covenants are strained and broken. The next ones explore what it might look like to rebuild them.

Third, they will turn toward action. Once you see the pattern, the natural question is now what? Later chapters will not offer a single master strategy, contexts differ too much for that, but they will draw on this playbook to suggest where different kinds of action matter most: when to defend courts, when to focus on local institutions, when to build broad coalitions, and when small persistent acts of refusal or solidarity can have outsized effects.

As you move forward, you do not need to carry every detail from this chapter with you. What matters most is the shape: that authoritarian drift is a process, not a single moment. That it works by combining emotional, institutional, and cultural moves. That it feeds on our understandable tendencies to normalize, delay, and turn against one another.

Keep that outline in the back of your mind. When later chapters talk about where your anger goes, what kinds of commitments hold under stress, and how collective action can still bend the story, it is this map they will be quietly referring back to.

Chapter References:
Bermeo, N. (2016). On democratic backsliding. Journal of Democracy, 27(1), 5-19.
Brookings Institution. (2025). Emergency powers and democratic erosion.
Carnegie Endowment for International Peace. (2025). States of emergency and the future of democracy.
Democratic Backsliding Panel. (2025). Democratic backsliding panel brief. University of Notre Dame.
Evans, R. J. (2005). The Coming of the Third Reich. Penguin.
Freedom House. (2022). Freedom in the World 2022: The global expansion of authoritarian rule.
Haggard, S., & Kaufman, R. R. (2021). Backsliding: Democratic regress in the contemporary world. Cambridge University Press.
Huq, A. Z., & Ginsburg, T. (2018). How to lose a constitutional democracy. UCLA Law Review, 65, 78-169.
Journal of Democracy. (2025). How to flip the script on the authoritarian playbook.
Levitsky, S., & Ziblatt, D. (2018). How Democracies Die. Crown.
Mettler, S., & Lieberman, R. C. (2020). Four Threats: The recurring crises of American democracy. St. Martin's Press.
Perez-Linan, A., et al. (2025). Democratic erosion in comparative perspective.
Protect Democracy. (2024). The Authoritarian Playbook (Updated ed.).
Straus, S. (2006). The Order of Genocide: Race, power, and war in Rwanda. Cornell University Press.
Svolik, M. W. (2012). The Politics of Authoritarian Rule. Cambridge University Press.
von Soest, C. (2025). Selective repression and regime survival.

3

SEEING THE PLAYBOOK IN ACTION

WHAT THE PATTERNS LOOKS LIKE IN REAL TIME

ONE PERSON STARTED COUNTING

Christina Pagel is a professor at University College London. Her formal title is Professor of Operational Research, which is a branch of applied mathematics used to solve real-world problems in healthcare systems. She has spent her career analyzing data, building models, and helping organizations see patterns in numbers that would otherwise remain invisible. She is not a political scientist. She is not an activist. She is someone who looks at complex information for a living and tries to make sense of it.

Her parents were German. Her father was born in 1937. Her mother was born in 1941. They grew up in a post-war Germany that was trying to reckon with how an educated, modern society had allowed itself to slide into fascism. That reckoning was the background noise of Pagel's childhood. Not as a formal lesson taught once and forgotten, but as a lived understanding carried by the people who raised her: democratic norms can collapse faster than anyone watching believes possible.

When Donald Trump began his second term in January 2025, Pagel did what came naturally. She opened a spreadsheet. She started writing down what the administration was doing, action by action, sourced to a news article each time. She was not trying to build anything public. She was trying to make sense of the sheer volume of what was happening. Executive orders. Firings. Institutional restructurings. Rhetorical escalations. Attacks on universities. Deportations. Threats against judges. Withdrawal from international agreements. The actions arrived faster than any single person could track, which was, as she would later note, part of the strategy.

Steve Bannon had said it plainly in 2018: the way to beat the media was to flood the zone with shit. The phrase was crude, but the logic was precise. When too much happens too fast, people cannot form a coherent picture of what is going on. Each action is covered individually, debated in isolation, and then pushed aside by the next one. No narrative holds. No pattern emerges. Accountability becomes impossible because no one can keep the full list in their heads long enough to draw conclusions from it.

Pagel's spreadsheet was her answer to that problem. She was not editorializing. She was cataloging.

By February 13, 2025, three weeks into the second term, she had logged 76 actions. She published an analysis on her Substack, titled with a line from a movie about a fictional republic that destroyed itself from within: "So this is how liberty dies." She mapped the 76 actions onto a Venn diagram organized around five broad domains that correspond to features of authoritarian states. She referenced the work of Steven Levitsky and Daniel Ziblatt, whose book How Democracies Die had outlined how modern democracies fail not through coups but through legal, incremental erosion.

CHAPTER 3

She referenced Timothy Snyder's The Road to Unfreedom, which documented the same patterns in Putin's Russia and Orban's Hungary.

The Venn diagram was dense. Even zoomed in, it was hard to read every entry. That was the point. Three weeks. 76 actions. Five overlapping domains of authoritarian behavior. And it was only the beginning.

Trump Action Tracker

Documenting the actions, statements, and plans of President Trump and his administration that echo those of authoritarian regimes and may pose a threat to American democracy, since January 2025

Total Actions	Violating Democratic Norms, Undermining Rule of Law	Hollowing State / Weaponizing Federal Institutions	Suppressing Dissent / Weaponizing State Against 'Enemies'
2455 Since January 2025	**Undermining Democracy** 663	**Hollowing State** 162	**Suppressing Dissent** 648
Controlling Information Including Spreading Misinformation and Propaganda	Control of Science & Health to Align with State Ideology	Attacking Universities, Schools, Museums, Culture	Weakening Civil Rights
Controlling Information 312	**Attacking Science** 404	**Attacking Education** 185	**Weakening Civil Rights** 433
Corruption & Enrichment	Aggressive Foreign Policy & Global Destabilization	Anti-immigrant or Militarized Nationalism	
Corruption 165	**Foreign Policy** 374	**Nationalism** 548	

THE SPREADSHEET THAT WOULD NOT STOP GROWING

Pagel kept counting. Every day, new actions arrived. Some were executive orders. Some were agency directives. Some were public statements or threats. Some were quiet personnel changes that only appeared in the news cycle for a few hours before being buried by the next round. She logged each one, assigned it to one or more of her five domains, and linked it to a published news source.

By the time she launched the Trump Action Tracker website in July 2025, the spreadsheet contained more than 740 entries. She had recruited two volunteers: Sandy Laping, a science communicator who helped track actions and maintain the data, and Pete Duncanson, a software developer who built the website in his spare time. Duncanson described his motivation simply. He wanted to sleep a little more soundly knowing he was at least doing something.

The site went live at TrumpActionTracker.info as a free, searchable, downloadable database. Every action included a date, a description, a source link, and domain assignments. Users could filter by time period, by domain, or by keyword. The full dataset could be downloaded as a CSV file under a Creative Commons license, meaning anyone could use it for research, journalism, or education.

By October 2025, the count had passed 1,600. Pagel expanded the original five domains into ten subcategories because the volume of actions had grown too large for the initial framework to capture meaningful distinctions. The Birkbeck University of London hosted a public conversation with Pagel about the project, listing the count at 1,460 at the time of its event announcement. By the time attendees arrived, the number had already climbed past that.

She also began producing short video and podcast updates, averaging about ten minutes each, covering actions that mainstream media had underreported or missed entirely. The University of California San Diego included the Trump Action Tracker in its official library guide to government information resources, alongside trackers maintained by major policy organizations, legal associations, and news outlets.

One mathematician with a spreadsheet had built what no newsroom or policy institute had managed to produce: a continuously updated, publicly accessible record of the full scope of what was happening, organized so that people could see not just individual events but the pattern those events formed together.

CHAPTER 3

Five Doors Into the Same Room

The previous chapter gave you a three-phase framework for understanding how authoritarian drift works in general. Pagel's five domains do something different. They give you a way to see that drift in real time, as it is happening, sorted not by phase but by the type of democratic function under attack.

These two frameworks are not in competition. They are complementary. The playbook in Chapter 2 tells you the shape of the story. Pagel's domains tell you which parts of the house are on fire right now. When you lay one over the other, the picture sharpens considerably.

What follows is a walk through each of the five original domains, not as an exhaustive catalog but as a lens for understanding what the tracker reveals about where the pressure is being applied.

Undermining democracy and the rule of law. This is the structural domain. It covers attacks on the machinery that makes self-governance possible: elections, courts, independent agencies, congressional oversight, constitutional limits on executive power, and access to public information. When Chapter 2 described Phase Two of the authoritarian playbook, the capture and tilting of institutions, this is the domain that tracks it.

The tracker documents actions like efforts to weaken judicial oversight, punish judges and prosecutors who issue unfavorable rulings, undermine the authority of Congress as a co-equal branch of government, and restrict public access to government data. It captures executive orders that expand presidential power into areas traditionally managed by independent agencies. It logs the firing or sidelining of inspectors general, the gutting of ethics offices, and the quiet rewriting of rules that determine how oversight bodies can investigate the executive branch.

What makes this domain so important is that it is foundational. When democratic checks and balances are weakened, every other abuse becomes easier. Courts that might block unconstitutional actions are defanged. Agencies that might expose corruption are dismantled or captured. The legislature is reduced to a spectator. The rule of law does not vanish overnight. It is hollowed out from the inside so that the structure remains standing while the substance is gone. That is precisely the pattern Chapter 2 described, and the tracker shows it happening one documented action at a time.

Dismantling social protections and civil rights. This domain tracks actions that target specific groups through policy, law enforcement, or rhetoric. Mass deportations. Restrictions on asylum. Rollbacks of civil rights protections for LGBTQ communities, women, and minority populations. Attacks on diversity and inclusion initiatives across government and the private sector. Policies that reduce due process protections for immigrants, including the detention and deportation of individuals on valid visas.

Authoritarian movements have always gained power by shrinking the circle of people who fully enjoy legal protections. This is not a coincidence. It is a mechanism. When certain groups are excluded from the community of people whose rights matter, two things happen simultaneously. First, the practical scope of legal accountability narrows, because enforcement becomes selective and politically directed. Second, a moral permission structure is created. If those people are not fully part of us, then what happens to them is not fully our concern. That logic, once established, never stays confined to its original target. The circle keeps shrinking.

The tracker captures this process with uncomfortable precision. Individual deportation cases are logged alongside broader policy shifts, not because each case is a major policy event but because

Pagel recognized the importance of bearing witness to individual stories while also tracking the escalation of enforcement. The accumulation of entries in this domain tells a story that no single news article can convey: the scope, the pace, and the direction of movement.

Suppressing dissent and controlling information. This domain includes actions against journalists, universities, watchdog organizations, and peaceful protesters. Limiting press access. Threatening reporters. Criminalizing protest. Misusing surveillance tools against domestic critics. Instituting loyalty tests for government employees. Weaponizing executive power against perceived enemies through investigations, lawsuits, revocation of security clearances, and public threats of retaliation.

Chapter 2 described this as one of the most reliable indicators of authoritarian acceleration: when a government moves from merely criticizing its opponents to actively punishing them for dissent. The tracker documents the shift in granular detail. It captures not just high-profile confrontations but the quieter actions that signal a change in climate: a visa revoked for a graduate student who participated in a protest, an executive order expanding surveillance authority, a press briefing rule change that restricts which outlets can attend, a lawsuit filed against a law firm that represented a government critic.

Controlling information and intimidating critics are classic tools for preventing accountability. When journalists face legal harassment for doing their jobs, when universities are threatened with funding cuts for hosting speakers the administration dislikes, when government employees are subjected to loyalty screenings based on their social media activity, the message travels far beyond the individuals targeted. The message is that the cost of speaking has gone up. People adjust. Self-censorship spreads. The space for genuine public debate contracts without any formal announcement that debate has been restricted.

Eroding science, education, and truth. This domain flags actions that sideline, distort, or suppress expert knowledge. Cutting or politicizing research programs. Manipulating public health guidance. Shutting down climate and health data collection. Reshaping school curricula to align with ideological goals. Defunding grants that target improving the health of marginalized populations. Attacking the independence of universities. Restricting research on topics that contradict state ideology, including climate change and vaccine effectiveness.

When governments replace evidence with propaganda, citizens lose the ability to make informed choices. This is not a side effect. It is an objective. Science is inherently threatening to concentrated power because it produces conclusions based on evidence rather than loyalty. A climate study that contradicts energy policy, an epidemiological finding that contradicts a public health directive, an economic analysis that contradicts a tariff rationale: these are not just inconveniences. They are challenges to the narrative that justifies the exercise of authority. Suppressing them is not anti-intellectual vandalism, though it may look that way. It is information warfare.

The tracker reveals something particularly striking in this domain: the breadth of the attack. It is not limited to one scientific field or one type of institution. The actions span cuts to infectious disease surveillance, elimination of environmental protections, restrictions on academic freedom, attacks on museums and cultural institutions, defunding of arts and humanities programs, and the removal of publicly accessible government data. Taken individually, each action can be framed as a budget decision or a policy preference. Taken together, they form a systematic effort to reshape what a society is allowed to know.

CHAPTER 3

Aggressive foreign policy and militarized nationalism. This domain captures actions that use military power, sanctions, and diplomatic pressure to consolidate power at home while reshaping the international environment. Threatening the sovereignty of allied nations. Withdrawing from international institutions like the World Health Organization and the Paris Climate Agreement. Undermining NATO. Using tariffs and trade policy as coercive tools. Deploying military-style enforcement within the United States through agencies like ICE and the National Guard. Demonizing immigrants through nationalist rhetoric. Celebrating dehumanizing conditions in detention facilities.

Authoritarian leaders have always used external enemies and strongman foreign policy to strengthen their domestic position. The logic is circular but effective: threats abroad justify expanded power at home, and expanded power at home is used to pursue more aggressive postures abroad. Nationalism provides the emotional fuel for both. When citizens are taught that their country is under siege from enemies within and without, the demand for a strong leader who does not tolerate dissent or constraint grows naturally.

By October 2025, Pagel found it necessary to split this domain into separate categories for aggressive foreign policy and militarized nationalism, because the volume and character of actions in each area had become distinct enough to warrant separate tracking. The deployment of ICE and National Guard units to American cities governed by political opponents, for instance, represented a different kind of action than the withdrawal from an international treaty, even though both fell under the broad umbrella of nationalist power projection.

Where the Domains Overlap

One of the most important findings in Pagel's data is that roughly half of all logged actions fall into two or more domains simultaneously. This is not a coding quirk. It is a reflection of how authoritarian systems actually work.

When the administration fires scientists at a federal health agency, that action hits science and education, democratic institutions, and social protections at the same time. When it deports a graduate student who participated in a campus protest, that action hits civil rights, suppression of dissent, and nationalism simultaneously. When it threatens a law firm for representing a government critic, that action hits rule of law, suppression of dissent, and the weaponization of state power against perceived enemies.

This overlap is the most important thing to see. Chapter 2 described the authoritarian playbook as a system of reinforcing actions where each move makes the next one easier. Pagel's data proves it. The overlapping domain assignments are not just a feature of how she categorized things. They are a feature of how the actions were designed. Multidomain actions are efficient. They accomplish several objectives at once, weaken multiple checks simultaneously, and make it harder for opposition to respond because the attack is coming from too many directions at once.

This is what Steve Bannon meant by flooding the zone. It is not just about volume. It is about complexity. When a single action damages three different democratic functions at once, and dozens of those actions arrive every week, the capacity of any institution, newsroom, or citizenry to respond coherently is overwhelmed. The sheer density of overlapping damage is itself a weapon.

CHAPTER 3

THE OVERVIEW GAP

Pagel has described the core problem her tracker addresses as an overview gap. Mainstream media covers individual actions. A policy here. A firing there. A lawsuit. A speech. A deportation. Each story is reported, debated, and then replaced by the next one. What is almost never shown is the full picture: how many actions have accumulated, which domains are being attacked most heavily, how the pace is changing over time, and where the overlaps concentrate.

This gap is not caused by laziness or incompetence. It is structural. News organizations are designed to cover events, not patterns. Each story must stand on its own. Each article needs a hook, a narrative arc, and a resolution. The authoritarian playbook exploits this by producing events faster than any narrative can contain them. No single article can convey that more than 1,600 documented actions, each with a news source, each assigned to at least one domain of authoritarian behavior, had accumulated in less than a year. The number itself is the story, and traditional news formats are not built to tell it.

The tracker fills that gap. It does not replace journalism. It provides a scaffold that makes journalism more legible. When a reporter covers a specific agency restructuring, the tracker shows you that this restructuring is one of dozens in the same domain, occurring alongside hundreds of other actions across related domains, accelerating rather than decelerating over time. Context changes interpretation. An isolated event can be rationalized. A documented pattern cannot.

Why Someone in London Had to Build This

There is something worth sitting with in the fact that this project was built by a British mathematician, not by an American institution. No major American university, newsroom, or policy organization produced a comprehensive, continuously updated, publicly searchable tracker of this scope during the period in question. Some built narrower trackers focused on specific areas like immigration enforcement, tariffs, censorship, or retaliatory investigations. The University of California San Diego compiled a library guide listing dozens of these individual trackers. But the broad, cross-domain view that Pagel built, the one that reveals how the actions reinforce one another across categories, came from outside the country.

That fact is not an indictment of American institutions. It is a demonstration of how proximity can limit perspective. When you are inside the flood, it is harder to see the shape of the water. Pagel had distance, both geographic and cultural. She also had a family history that inoculated her against the assumption that it cannot happen here. Her parents had grown up in a country that proved, catastrophically, that it could.

The lesson is not that Americans need outsiders to do their thinking for them. The lesson is that pattern recognition sometimes requires stepping back far enough to see the whole board. And that when someone does that work, the appropriate response is not embarrassment but gratitude, and then the decision to use what they have built.

What This Means for You

Chapter 2 gave you a map. This chapter showed you someone who used it.

CHAPTER 3

Pagel did not have special authority. She was not a government official, a political operative, or a professional activist. She was a mathematician with a spreadsheet, a set of references, and the discipline to keep counting when the numbers became overwhelming. The tracker exists because she refused to accept the two most common responses to political overload: looking away and assuming someone else would handle it.

If you have read Chapter 2 and this chapter back to back, you now have both the theoretical framework and the empirical evidence. You know the phases. You know the domains. You know that roughly half the documented actions hit multiple domains simultaneously. You know the pace is accelerating rather than slowing. You know that what you have been feeling is not paranoia and not partisanship. It is pattern recognition, and it is supported by data.

The question that follows is the one that every chapter in this book eventually arrives at: now what?

Knowing the pattern is not the same as changing it. Understanding the playbook does not by itself make the playbook stop working. But it does change your relationship to it. You stop arguing about whether each individual action is really that bad and start asking whether the overall direction is acceptable. You stop waiting for the single dramatic moment that proves democracy is in danger and start paying attention to the accumulation of smaller moves that collectively produce that danger. You stop feeling crazy for noticing what others seem willing to ignore.

The chapters ahead will turn toward what to do with that clarity. How to manage the anger that comes with it without letting it consume you. How to think about the commitments that hold societies together and what it takes to rebuild them when they fray. How to act, individually and collectively, in ways that address the pattern rather than just the latest headline.

But before we get there, take a moment to appreciate what Pagel demonstrated. The playbook depends on your inability to see the whole picture. When someone assembles that picture and makes it available, the playbook loses some of its power. Not all of it. But enough to matter. Enough to change the conversation from did that really happen to here is everything that happened, sourced and organized, and you can verify it yourself. That shift, from confusion to clarity, from isolation to shared reality, is one of the most important things a citizen can contribute.

You do not need to build a tracker. But you do need to stop pretending the pattern is not there. The data exists. The map exists. What happens next depends on what people do with both.

Chapter References:

Pagel, C. (2025, February 13). "So this is how liberty dies..." Making sense of Trump's first three weeks. Substack: Making sense... of evidence, data, and the stories they tell. https://christinapagel.substack.com/p/so-this-is-how-liberty-dies-making

Pagel, C. (2025, July). Introducing the Trump Action Tracker website! Substack: Making sense... of evidence, data, and the stories they tell. https://christinapagel.substack.com/p/introducing-the-trump-action-tracker

Pagel, C. (2025, October 26). The Trump Action Tracker has had an update! Substack: Making sense... of evidence, data, and the stories they tell. https://christinapagel.substack.com/p/the-trump-action-tracker-has-had

Trump Action Tracker. About page: project origin, motivations, domains, team, and domain allocation methodology. https://www.trumpactiontracker.info/about

Trump Action Tracker. Main database. https://www.trumpactiontracker.info/

Birkbeck, University of London. (2025). What Is Trump doing to Democracy? In Conversation with Professor Christina Pagel. Event listing. https://www.bbk.ac.uk/events/

Rhyming Chaos podcast. (2025, August 22). A mathematician looks at Trump's authoritarian takeover. Interview with Christina Pagel. https://www.rhymingchaos.com/p/a-mathematician-looks-at-trumps-authoritarian

University of California San Diego Libraries. Trump Trackers. U.S. Government Information LibGuide. https://ucsd.libguides.com/usgov/trumptrackers

Levitsky, S., & Ziblatt, D. (2018). How Democracies Die. Crown.

Snyder, T. (2018). The Road to Unfreedom: Russia, Europe, America. Tim Duggan Books.

Applebaum, A. (2020). Twilight of Democracy: The Seductive Lure of Authoritarianism. Doubleday.

Policy Commons. Trump Action Tracker organizational listing. https://policycommons.net/orgs/trump-action-tracker/

4

HOW TO SHAPE ANGER TO THE UNIQUE YOU

Anger Is a Signal, Not a Script

*A*nger is not the thing that breaks people. What breaks people is having nowhere to put it.

Most of us were never taught what anger is for. We were taught to suppress it, moralize it, joke about it, or explode with it. Very rarely were we taught how to use it. So when anger shows up, especially the kind that comes from watching something unjust unfold slowly and repeatedly, it often turns inward or sideways. People feel restless, tense, distracted, and overwhelmed, but also strangely frozen. That is not a personal weakness. It is a design flaw in how we talk about civic responsibility.

Anger is a signal. It tells you that something you value is being violated. It does not tell you what to do next. When people mistake anger for action, they burn out or act recklessly. When people are told that anger itself is wrong, they disengage and go numb. Both outcomes serve systems that want people exhausted, divided, or silent.

The question is not how to calm down. The question is how to translate anger into sustained, constructive action without losing yourself in the process.

That translation looks different depending on who you are. There is no single right response. There never has been. A thinker who processes anger by mapping patterns needs a different channel than a storyteller who processes anger by making people feel what she feels. A protector who responds by scanning for who is vulnerable needs a different outlet than a connector who responds by pulling people together. If you try to force everyone through the same funnel, the anger either stalls or detonates.

This chapter does two things. First, it helps you identify your own shape: the natural way you respond to injustice, the strengths that shape has, and the specific actions it can fuel. Second, it shows how different shapes fit together, because anger channeled alone burns fast, while anger coordinated across complementary roles builds something that lasts.

Before people act together, they need to understand themselves. Otherwise they imitate whoever is loudest, take risks they are not prepared for, or confuse adrenaline with strategy.

The Movement Ecosystem

Every serious movement that has endured long enough to matter has relied on more than one kind of person. Not because diversity is a pleasant idea, but because the work itself has multiple dimensions, and no single temperament can cover them all.

Researchers studying the structure of successful social movements, from the American civil rights campaigns to the anti-apartheid struggle in South Africa to the Solidarity movement in Poland, have consistently found that durable resistance draws on a range of complementary roles. Erica Chenoweth's landmark research on nonviolent resistance, published in her 2011 study with Maria Stephan, demonstrated that the single most reliable predictor of a movement's success was broad participation across demographic groups and skill sets, not the charisma of a single leader or the drama of a single confrontation.

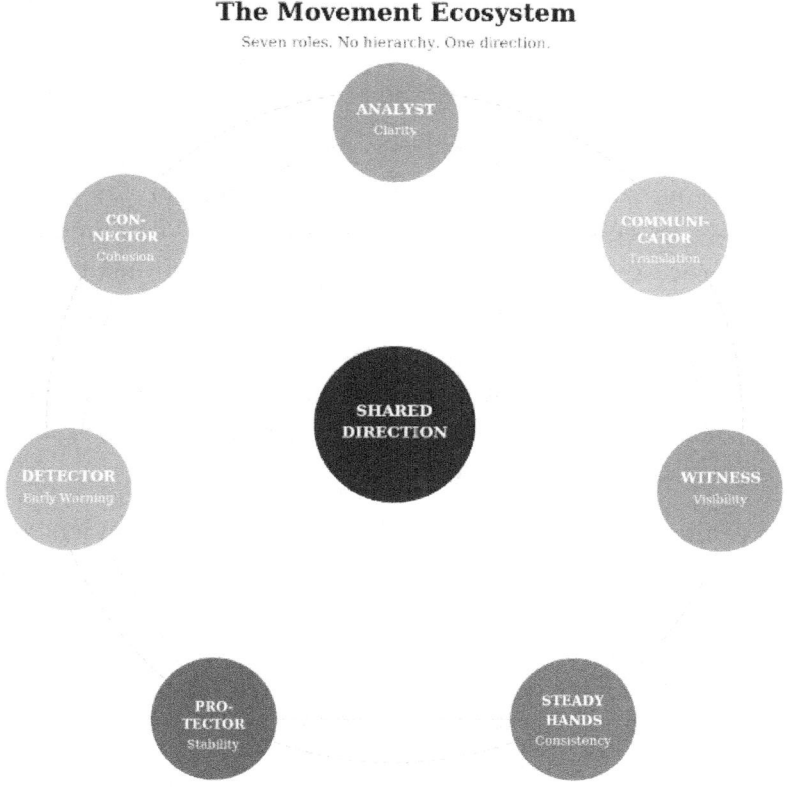

The Movement Ecosystem

Seven roles. No hierarchy. One direction.

Every role feeds the others. No single role sustains the whole.

What follows is a map of seven roles that appear, under different names, in nearly every effective collective effort. These are not personality tests. They are functional descriptions. You may recognize yourself in more than one. You may shift between them over time. What matters is that you can locate yourself honestly, because that is how anger stops being a weight and starts becoming a contribution.

The Analyst

Core strength: Clarity

Some people respond to chaos by trying to understand it. They read deeply, connect patterns, notice inconsistencies, and feel unsettled until things make sense. These are the people who ask, "How did this actually happen?" and "What does this lead to if it continues?"

If this is you, your anger sharpens into focus. What you can do right now is slow the narrative down. Write. Map timelines. Explain processes in plain language. Translate legal or institutional changes into real-world effects people can grasp. When confusion spreads, people like you anchor reality. This work does not require visibility. It requires precision and patience. Much of what eventually becomes common knowledge starts as something one careful person bothered to explain clearly.

What drains you: Being rushed into action before you understand the situation. Environments where speed is valued over accuracy. Groups that treat your caution as indecision.

The Communicator

Core strength: Translation

Some people instinctively know how to speak to others in a way that lands. They feel the emotional temperature of a room. They can tell when someone is shutting down, defensive, or overwhelmed. They know how to say hard things without making people feel attacked.

If this is you, your anger turns into language that others can hold. What you can do is help ideas travel. You can talk to family members who would never attend a meeting. You can explain what is happening without sounding alarmist or condescending. You can keep conversations open that would otherwise close. Movements collapse when they only talk to themselves. Communicators keep the circle wide enough to matter.

What drains you: Being asked to simplify things so far that the truth gets lost. Feeling responsible for everyone's emotional reaction. Groups that mistake persuasion for compromise.

The Connector

Core strength: Cohesion

Some people naturally notice relationships. They see who is isolated, who is burned out, who needs support, and who should probably know each other. They create informal networks without calling them that. People trust them.

If this is you, your anger becomes a pull toward gathering. What you can do is keep people connected when systems are trying to isolate them. Organize dinners. Check in quietly. Introduce people working on similar things. Make sure no one disappears without someone noticing. Authoritarian systems depend on fragmentation. Community builders make resistance harder to fracture.

What drains you: Holding everyone else together while no one holds you. Being invisible in the work you do. Groups that treat relationship maintenance as optional.

The Detector

Core strength: Early warning

Some people are attuned to systems rather than speeches. They notice changes in rules, budgets, timelines, and processes. They read footnotes. They ask how decisions are actually made. They sense when the machinery of governance is being quietly rearranged while everyone is watching the spectacle.

If this is you, your anger takes the form of documentation. What you can do is keep records. Monitor policy changes. Pay attention to who is appointed where and with what authority. Preserve documentation. When people later ask, "When did this start?" you will have an answer. This kind of work rarely gets applause. It often becomes invaluable later.

What drains you: Sounding alarms that nobody responds to. Being told you are "reading too much into things." Groups that only pay attention to what is already on fire.

The Witness

Core strength: Visibility

Some people do not freeze when attention turns toward them. They can speak publicly, be recorded, be criticized, and still stay grounded. This does not mean they enjoy it. It means they can tolerate it.

If this is you, your anger becomes presence. What you can do is take on visibility so others do not have to. This might mean speaking to media, posting publicly, or showing up in spaces where silence would be interpreted as consent. Not everyone should do this. But when no one does, fear spreads faster than truth.

What drains you: Being treated as the face of a movement without the support behind it. Being expected to absorb hostility indefinitely. Groups that confuse your tolerance for pressure with invulnerability.

The Protector

Core strength: Stability

Some people move toward instability with a steady presence. They notice escalation. They think about safety, boundaries, and care. They are the ones who ask, "Who might get hurt?" and "What happens if this goes wrong?"

If this is you, your anger shows up as vigilance. What you can do is protect the human fabric of movements. That can mean legal observing, emotional support, safety planning, or simply being the person who checks in afterward. Movements fail not only from repression, but from exhaustion and neglect.

What drains you: Being cast as the person who always says no. Watching others take risks without preparation. Groups that treat caution as cowardice.

The Steady Hands

Core strength: Consistency

Many people read lists like the ones above and think none of it applies to them. They believe resistance requires bravery, charisma, or expertise they do not have. This belief is understandable. It is also false.

If this is you, your anger is quiet but durable. What you can do is show up. Reliably, without drama, doing one or two things that keep the larger effort alive. You vote consistently. You donate modestly and regularly. You volunteer for the unglamorous logistics that keep events and organizations running. You model integrity at work and at home. You hold your non-negotiables even when no one is watching. Most real change comes from people who show up consistently, not dramatically. From people who refuse to disappear. From people who do one or two things reliably and let that be enough.

What drains you: Being made to feel that your contributions do not count unless they are visible. Cultures that equate volume with commitment. Groups that celebrate the dramatic and forget the dependable.

Finding Your Shape

You do not need to choose one role permanently. Life changes. Your capacity changes. The situation changes. But it is useful, right now, to make a provisional identification, because people who know their shape are less likely to drift into someone else's and burn out trying to be something they are not.

Some questions that can help:

• When I hear bad news, what is my first instinct? Do I want to understand, to speak, to gather people, to check the details, to be seen, to protect, or to just keep doing what I am doing?

• In past moments of stress or conflict, what role did I naturally fall into? What did people come to me for?

• What kind of work energizes me even when the topic is painful? What kind of work leaves me feeling emptied rather than tired?

• What is the thing I keep doing even when no one asks me to?

If you can answer those honestly, you probably already know your shape. The point is not to limit yourself. It is to stop wasting energy pretending to be something you are not and start investing it where it actually multiplies.

Anger becomes destructive when it floats without purpose. It becomes useful when it sharpens attention and commitment. Your shape is where that sharpening happens.

When Many Shapes Move Together

Understanding yourself is necessary. It is not sufficient. At some point, the question shifts from "What is my shape?" to "How does my shape fit alongside others?"

This is where most people hesitate. Groups do not fail only because the problem is too big. They also fail because people are not sure how to be themselves inside something larger. They are afraid of being swallowed, corrected, or shamed. They are afraid that joining means erasing their nuances, their doubts, or their limits. So they stay on the edge, caring deeply, watching closely, and moving rarely.

The antidote is not forced unity. It is coordinated difference.

In real movements that last, you will find people who lead with analysis, people who lead with emotion, people who organize logistics, people who make art, people who protect, and people who simply keep showing up. When those roles are honored instead of ranked, when no single style is treated as the "real" way to care, groups become harder to break.

Most groups say they want "everyone," but in practice they often reward just a few types of contribution: the loudest voices, the people who are most comfortable with conflict, or the ones who can give the most time. That is how movements drift toward burnout and sameness. If you look at efforts that have held together under pressure, from the Solidarity trade union movement in Poland to the Otpor student resistance in Serbia to the broad coalitions behind the Indian independence movement, you almost always find at least four functions present, even if they go

CHAPTER 4

by different names: people who see clearly, people who help ideas travel, people who knit relationships, and people who step forward when visibility and risk are unavoidable. No single person can do all of these well at once. Groups that pretend otherwise burn people out. Groups that acknowledge these different functions and treat them as interdependent tend to last longer and adapt better.

THE THREE CORE TENSIONS

When many different shapes move together, friction is inevitable. But friction is not the same as failure. It is often a sign that a group has the right mix of people, and that they have not yet learned to name what is happening between them.

Across different movements, countries, and eras, three tensions appear with striking regularity. They are not problems to be solved. They are balances to be managed.

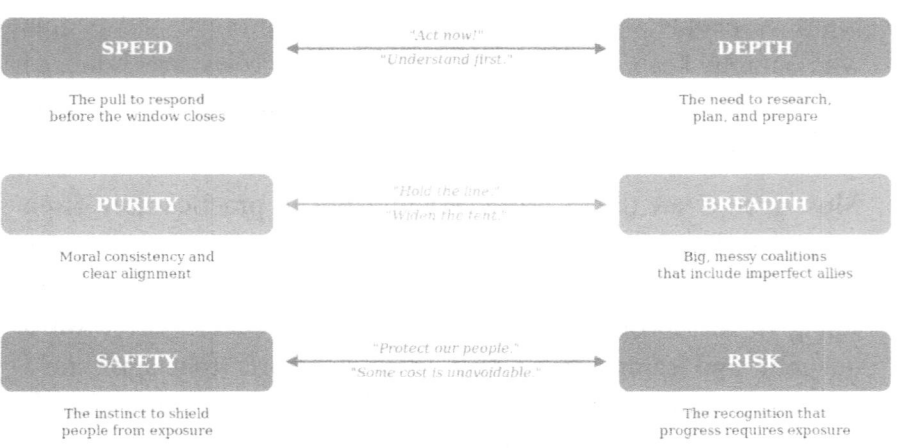

Speed versus depth. Analysts get frustrated when groups rush to action before understanding the terrain. Communicators and witnesses get frustrated when groups study so long the moment passes. Both are right. The tension itself is productive. A group that only studies never moves. A group that only moves never learns. What matters is whether the group can name where it is leaning and adjust, rather than treating one pole as the permanent correct answer.

Purity versus breadth. Some members want the group's message to be morally clean and its boundaries clear. Others want the coalition as wide as possible, even if that means including people whose agreement is partial or whose past record is imperfect. This tension appears in every significant movement in recorded history. The Indian National Congress struggled with it. The American civil rights movement struggled with it. Modern climate movements struggle with it. There is no permanent resolution. The question is always contextual: right now, in this situation, does the greater danger come from diluting our principles or from shrinking our numbers?

Safety versus risk. Protectors naturally emphasize what could go wrong. Witnesses and organizers often push for actions that require some exposure. Neither instinct is wrong. A group paralyzed by caution never creates the openings that change calculations. A group that ignores safety burns through people faster than it can replace them. The healthiest groups hold both voices and let the situation, not the loudest personality, determine where the dial sits.

Groups get into trouble when they treat these tensions as battles to be won rather than balances to be managed. When one pole is declared the "right" one, always faster, always broader, always safer, whole kinds of people start to feel like a problem instead of a contribution. A more honest way to work is to name the tension out loud: "We need someone slowing us down and someone pushing us forward. We need people guarding red lines and people building bridges." Once roles are named, disagreement becomes easier to place. Not "you are wrong," but "right now we are leaning so far in your direction that we are losing sight of the other need."

Finding Your Place Without Disappearing

Joining with others does not mean abandoning your boundaries. In fact, those boundaries are what make durable collaboration possible.

When people ignore their own limits, they often compensate later with resentment. They say yes to every request, volunteer for every role, and then vanish when it becomes too much. They agree publicly and disagree privately. They stay silent until something small becomes the last straw. From the outside, this looks like flakiness. From the inside, it feels like self-protection that came too late.

You are allowed to be explicit about what you can and cannot do. You can say, "I can help with research, but I cannot lead meetings." You can say, "I can show up at protests twice a month, but not every week." You can say, "I can host, but I cannot speak," or "I can speak, but I need someone else to handle logistics." When you name this clearly, you are not being selfish. You are making it easier for groups to plan realistically instead of relying on invisible labor and unspoken expectations. You are also giving other people permission to be honest about their own limits.

The point is to offer your shape on purpose, not to squeeze yourself into whatever space is loudest at the moment.

One of the quiet fears that keeps people from joining collective efforts is the fear of being swallowed. They have watched groups where everyone starts to sound the same, where doubt is treated as betrayal, where internal culture feels as rigid as the thing they are resisting. They would rather act alone than lose their own voice.

You do not have to give up your distinctness to act with others. But you may need to decide where you will bend and where you will not. If a group constantly demands that you deny what you see, laugh at what you find cruel, or take risks you have clearly said you cannot take, that is not a healthy place for you. Leaving is not a failure. It is a way of protecting the part of you that can still act elsewhere. At the same time, if every disagreement feels like an attack on your identity, collaboration becomes impossible. You will need to distinguish between moments when your integrity is genuinely threatened and moments when you are simply uncomfortable because someone else's shape differs from yours. That discernment is part of staying yourself without standing alone.

When Groups Get Sick

Not every group that claims to resist authoritarianism is healthy. Some replicate the very dynamics they are trying to oppose: rigid hierarchy, enforced conformity, punishment of dissent, and the celebration of sacrifice over sustainability. It is possible to build something that fights the right enemy and still destroys the people inside it.

The following diagnostic is not a formal assessment. It is a set of contrasts that can help you recognize whether a group you are part of, or considering joining, is functioning or fracturing. Three or more signs on the left side suggest that the group's internal structure needs attention before its external mission can succeed.

CHAPTER 4

Group Health Diagnostic

Warning signs on the left. Healthy signs on the right.

FRACTURING	FUNCTIONING
One voice dominates Same person speaks at every meeting, sets every agenda, gets final say	**Leadership rotates** Different people facilitate, speak publicly, and set direction over time
Doubt is treated as disloyalty Questions get shut down; people learn to perform agreement	**Doubt is welcomed as input** Concerns are heard; people can disagree without being punished
Burnout is normalized Exhaustion is worn as a badge; rest is seen as weakness	**Rest is built into the rhythm** Breaks are planned, not punished; stepping back is supported
Only one type of action counts Protests are "real" work; research, care, and logistics are overlooked	**Multiple contributions are honored** Research, care, logistics, and visibility are treated as equal
People vanish without notice Members quietly disappear; no one checks in or asks what happened	**Absences are noticed and met gently** Someone reaches out; return is welcomed without guilt or judgment
Internal conflict turns personal Disagreements become character attacks; factions form quietly	**Friction is named and placed** Tensions are discussed as role collisions, not personal failures
Sacrifice is the unspoken standard Those who give the most are "real"; everyone else feels inadequate	**Sustainability is the actual standard** The group measures health by who is still here, not who burned brightest

If your group shows warning signs, the response is not necessarily to leave. It may be to name what you see. Many groups drift into dysfunction not out of malice but out of urgency. They skip the work of building healthy internal culture because the external threat feels too pressing to slow down for. That is understandable. It is also how movements eat themselves.

The people who notice these patterns earliest are often the connectors and protectors. They feel the temperature of the room. They notice when someone goes quiet. They sense when exhaustion is being mistaken for commitment. If this is your shape, your willingness to name what you see is not a distraction from the mission. It is what keeps the mission alive.

Moving in the Same Direction

Coming together does not require perfect agreement. It requires enough shared direction that your different efforts add up instead of canceling out.

In practice, that often means answering a few simple questions together. What, exactly, are we trying to stop or change? What are we trying to protect or build in its place? Over the next season, what are the one or two pressure points where our combined effort might matter most?

The answers do not need to be forever. They need to be clear enough for now that people can orient their particular gifts toward a common horizon. Analysts can focus their research on those pressure points. Communicators can craft language that connects them to everyday life. Organizers can design actions that match the group's real capacity. Protectors can anticipate where stress will fall hardest. Witnesses can decide when and how to step forward so others do not have to. Detectors can track whether the pressure is having an effect or whether the target has shifted. Steady hands can sustain the unglamorous daily work that keeps the effort from stalling between dramatic moments.

You will still disagree about strategy. You will still make mistakes. You will still misread each other at times. But you will be arguing inside a shared frame, rather than fighting over entirely different maps.

What This Chapter Sets Up

This chapter has moved through three layers: understanding anger as a signal, identifying the shape that determines how your anger translates into action, and seeing how different shapes can work together without destroying each other or themselves.

CHAPTER 4

If it worked, you should not feel pressured to do everything. You should feel clearer about what you can do next. You should have a provisional sense of your own role, a realistic picture of what groups need, language for the frictions that arise when roles interact, and permission to participate without disappearing.

The chapters ahead move closer to the ground, including how to apply real pressure without becoming the damage, choosing your risk level and build support around it, and what happens when the fight gets longer and harder than you expected.

But the foundation underneath all of those chapters is this one. You cannot apply pressure well if you do not know your shape. You cannot choose your risk level honestly if you have not named your limits. You cannot hold the line over time if you are performing someone else's courage instead of exercising your own.

Anger is not the enemy. Directionless anger is. You now have a direction. *Many shapes. One direction.*

Chapter References:
  Ackerman, P., & DuVall, J. (2000). A force more powerful: A century of nonviolent conflict. Palgrave Macmillan.
  Boulding, E. (2000). Cultures of peace: The hidden side of history. Syracuse University Press.
  Chenoweth, E., & Stephan, M. J. (2011). Why civil resistance works: The strategic logic of nonviolent conflict. Columbia University Press.
  Ganz, M. (2009). Why David sometimes wins: Leadership, organization, and strategy in the California farm worker movement. Oxford University Press.
  Han, H. (2014). How organizations develop activists: Civic associations and leadership in the 21st century. Oxford University Press.
  Maslach, C., & Leiter, M. P. (2016). Burnout. In G. Fink (Ed.), Stress: Concepts, cognition, emotion, and behavior (pp. 351-357). Academic Press.
  McAdam, D. (1982). Political process and the development of Black insurgency, 1930-1970. University of Chicago Press.
  Nepstad, S. E. (2011). Nonviolent revolutions: Civil resistance in the late 20th century. Oxford University Press.

Popovic, S., & Miller, M. (2015). Blueprint for revolution: How to use rice pudding, Lego men, and other nonviolent techniques to galvanize communities, overthrow dictators, or simply change the world. Spiegel and Grau.

Sharp, G. (1973). The politics of nonviolent action (3 vols.). Porter Sargent.

Tarrow, S. (2011). Power in movement: Social movements and contentious politics (3rd ed.). Cambridge University Press.

Tilly, C., & Tarrow, S. (2015). Contentious politics (2nd ed.). Oxford University Press.

5

APPLYING PRESSURE WITHOUT BECOMING THE DAMAGE

Authoritarian systems are not just hoping you will do nothing. They are also hoping that, if you do act, you will do it in ways that confirm their story: that you are dangerous, reckless, cruel, or easily dismissed. They want you either absent or over the line.

This chapter is about the space in between.

It is about how to apply real pressure, pressure that can change calculations, not just express feelings, without losing the moral and strategic ground you still have. It is about raising the cost of abuse without escalating harm. It is about remembering that *how* you fight shapes what you are fighting for.

Pressure That Works Versus Pressure That Feels Good

Not all pressure is the same.

Some actions are emotionally satisfying but strategically thin. They let people vent, signal belonging, or feel briefly powerful, but they do not actually change incentives for those in power. Other actions may be less dramatic but do more to alter what leaders, institutions, or enablers can safely do.

A good test is simple:

- Does this action change what someone with power **risks**, **needs**, or **expects**?
- Or does it only change how *we* feel for a moment?

Marches, boycotts, sit-ins, strikes, noise campaigns, legal challenges, documentation, even infiltration can all matter. They matter most when they are tied to clear pressure points: a decision that needs to be stopped, a company that needs to withdraw support, an institution that needs to enforce its own rules, a public that needs to see what is being done in its name.

If you keep that in view, you are less likely to mistake catharsis for strategy.

The Case for Disruption and Its Limits

Authoritarian projects rely on people adapting to the abnormal. One way to resist is to refuse that adaptation: to disrupt routines so that the cost of "business as usual" rises.

Disruption is not a tantrum. It is a signal that something is wrong enough that normal operations cannot continue unchallenged.

Done well, disruption:

- Forces attention where it has been avoided.

- Shows that there are real numbers behind an objection, not just isolated complaints.
- Pressures specific decision-makers by interrupting the comfort or profits they rely on.

Done poorly, disruption:

- Punishes people who have little to do with the harm.
- Confirms the regime's narrative that opponents are irrational or dangerous.
- Burns through public sympathy faster than it builds power.

The difference is rarely about how loud or visible an action is. It is about whether it is *aimed*.

Blocking access to a government building during a crucial vote sends a different message than randomly vandalizing unrelated property. Targeted economic disruption of companies that profit directly from repression sends a different message than generalized chaos in neighborhoods that are already struggling. Loud, sustained protest outside the homes or offices of those implementing abusive policies sends a different message than harassing their children or neighbors.

The question is not "Is this disruptive?" but "Disruptive to *whom*, and toward *what* end?"

Nonviolent Pressure: Why It Matters

Nonviolence is not passivity. It is a strategic and moral choice about how to wield power.

On the strategic side, nonviolent campaigns tend to:

- Attract broader participation, including people who would never join armed struggle.
- Make it easier for insiders, civil servants, security forces, business elites, to defect or refuse orders.
- Lower the justification for harsh crackdowns in the eyes of the wider public and international observers.

On the moral side, nonviolence is about refusing to reproduce the dynamics you are trying to end: the idea that might makes right, that some lives are expendable, that fear is a legitimate governing tool. It is about drawing a line you will not cross, even when others already have.

This does not mean nonviolent pressure is gentle. It can be sharp, costly, and sustained. It can shut down ports, delay flights, interrupt supply chains, halt daily routines, and confront people with what they would rather not see. What it does not do is treat other human beings as acceptable collateral.

Whenever you are unsure where the line is, you can return to a simple question: "If everyone used this tactic against those they oppose, would the world be more or less like the one we are trying to build?"

Protest: Presence That Changes the Math

Protest is often the first tool people think of and the easiest to dismiss. Rallies alone rarely topple regimes. They can, however, shift calculations when they are sustained, strategic, and connected to other forms of pressure.

Protest is most powerful when it:

- Shows that opposition is broad, not confined to a few stereotypes.
- Signals to would-be allies inside institutions that they will not stand alone if they resist.
- Raises the reputational cost of abusive policies for those implementing them.

To keep protest from becoming empty ritual, groups can:

- Tie major demonstrations to specific decision points, votes, appointments, contracts, crackdowns, rather than scattering energy.
- Pair street presence with follow-up: legal challenges, media outreach, direct pressure on officials.
- Plan for sustainability: rotating roles, clear safety plans, emotional support, and realistic expectations about what one march can and cannot do.

Protest does not have to be polite. It does have to be purposeful.

Boycotts and Economic Pressure: Moving the Money

Power is not only held by politicians. It is held by companies, investors, donors, and institutions that profit from or stabilize abusive systems. Boycotts and economic pressure target those pillars.

A well-aimed boycott:

- Names the specific behavior that is unacceptable (e.g., providing technology for surveillance, profiting from detention, sponsoring propaganda).

- Identifies the actors who could change it (company leadership, investors, clients).
- Offers a clear path for exiting the boycott (what must change for pressure to stop).

This is different from unfocused calls to "boycott everything." Overly broad campaigns may feel righteous but often dilute leverage.

Economic pressure can also work in the opposite direction: "buycotts" that deliberately support businesses, media, and organizations that uphold democratic norms. Money is a signal. Where you withdraw it and where you place it both matter.

The aim is not to ruin as many people as possible. It is to create a clear choice for those standing on the fence: continue supporting abuse and accept growing costs, or step away and retain legitimacy and custom.

Refusal and Noncooperation: Saying No From Inside

Many of the most powerful levers are held by people inside systems: civil servants, local officials, health workers, educators, union members, tech staff, contractors, clergy. When they refuse to cooperate with abuse, especially in numbers, the machinery grinds.

Noncooperation can look like:

- Workers refusing to carry out orders that clearly violate rights or law.
- Professionals refusing to lend their expertise to legitimize sham processes.

- Religious or community leaders declining to bless policies that scapegoat or dehumanize.
- Contractors walking away from deals that directly support repression.

These choices carry risk. No one should be pushed into them lightly. But when insiders act together, through unions, professional associations, or informal networks, they can raise the cost of abusive policies more quickly than any outside protest.

The key is to pair refusal with visibility and support. People who say no need legal backup where possible, emotional and practical support, and public acknowledgment. Otherwise, their sacrifice disappears into the news cycle, and others learn that resistance means isolation.

Documentation and Exposure: Turning Light Into Leverage

Authoritarian systems rely on two things at once: control and plausible deniability. They want the power to act and the ability to say, "That's not really happening," or "It's not as bad as you think."

Careful documentation undercuts that deniability.

This includes:

- Recording abuses when it is safe to do so.
- Keeping copies of orders, policies, and directives.
- Logging changes to rules, budgets, and appointments over time.
- Preserving testimony from those directly affected.

Documentation by itself does not stop harm, but it changes the terrain. It provides raw material for legal challenges, journalism, international pressure, and later accountability. It also protects your own side from sliding into rumor and exaggeration, which can be easily discredited.

The discipline here is to tell the truth even when it is tempting to embellish. Accuracy is not politeness. It is your best armor.

Strikes: When Work Stops

Strikes are one of the most powerful tools ordinary people have, because they directly affect what regimes and their backers care about: economic output, social stability, and international reputation.

They can range from short, symbolic stoppages to prolonged, sector-wide shutdowns. They are also high-risk, especially in contexts without strong labor protections or where regimes have shown willingness to retaliate brutally.

Strikes work best when:

- They are clearly tied to specific, achievable demands.
- They are organized through structures that can support participants, strike funds, mutual aid, legal assistance.
- They are coordinated across sectors where possible, so pressure is not easily isolated.
- Participants understand both the risks and the plan for de-escalation if demands are met.

The line to watch is between targeting systems and harming people who are already vulnerable. A strike that shuts down luxury services has a different moral weight than one that blocks access to critical medicine or food. Where essential services are involved, partial or rotating strikes may be more ethical and more sustainable.

CHAPTER 5

INFILTRATION AND INSIDE GAME: USING THE DOORS THAT EXIST

Sometimes the most effective way to block harmful moves is from inside parties, institutions, or organizations that are drifting toward authoritarian behavior. This can mean joining political parties to vote in primaries, running for internal offices, or taking roles in civic bodies that still have some autonomy.

Infiltration in this sense is not about deception for its own sake. It is about recognizing that if only the most extreme voices participate in certain spaces, those spaces will move further out of balance. When more moderate, principled people show up and stay, they can:

- Block the worst proposals.
- Support or elevate less extreme candidates.
- Slow or complicate attempts to rewrite rules.
- Bring information back out to those organizing on the outside.

This path is not for everyone. It demands patience, thick skin, and a tolerance for compromise. It can also be emotionally taxing to sit in rooms where decisions are made that you strongly oppose. But for some people and contexts, this "inside game" is a crucial part of raising the cost of hardline plans.

What matters is transparency with yourself: Why am I here? What are my red lines? Who am I accountable to outside this room? Without those anchors, the risk of being slowly co-opted is real.

Noise: Refusing to Let Abuse Be Comfortable

Sometimes the goal is not to stop a decision directly but to make it impossible for those carrying it out to feel that nothing is wrong. This is where "noise" comes in: protest and presence directed at specific sites and people, over time.

Noise can mean:

- Demonstrations outside detention centers so that those inside hear they are not forgotten.
- Vigils or loud protests at hotels, homes, or offices hosting those who are enforcing harmful policies.
- Coordinated call-in or write-in campaigns that flood offices with messages they cannot ignore.

The aim is not to harass families or random neighbors. It is to puncture the bubble of comfort that allows people to pretend their role is neutral. You are saying, "You can do this, but you cannot do it quietly."

As always, the line is about **direction and dignity**. Noise targeted at the responsible decision-makers, without dragging children, bystanders, or scapegoated communities into the fire, keeps pressure where it belongs.

Staying Human While Applying Pressure

The thread running through all of this is simple and hard: apply pressure in ways that bring you **closer** to the kind of society you want, not closer to the one you fear.

You will make mistakes. You will misjudge what works. You will sometimes aim too narrowly or too broadly. You will sometimes be tempted to answer cruelty with cruelty, contempt with contempt. The work is to notice those moments, course-correct, and keep asking:

- Does this action increase or decrease the space for truth, dignity, and shared rules?
- Am I treating anyone as expendable who is not?
- If this tactic became normal on all sides, would it help or harm the world we are trying to build?

Applying pressure without becoming the damage is not about being gentle. It is about being deliberate. It is about remembering that the point is not just to stop something bad, but to practice something better in real time.

The next chapter will turn more directly to protection: how people can shield one another from retaliation, burnout, and isolation while they do this work, so that resistance does not only spark, it endures.

6

CHOOSING YOUR LANE AND YOUR RISK

*E*very struggle has two maps: one of tactics, and one of people. You can know a hundred ways to apply pressure and still feel paralyzed if you are not honest about what you can actually risk.

This chapter is about that honesty.

It is not about grading your courage. It is about protecting you, and the movements you care about, from guilt, panic, and purity tests that do more harm than good.

Why Risk Is Not a Moral Scorecard

When things feel urgent, it is easy to start ranking people by how much danger they are willing to face. Those who take big risks are treated as heroes. Those who move more cautiously are treated as if they are less committed, less serious, or less pure.

That way of thinking may feel righteous. It is also false.

CHAPTER 6

People live under different conditions. Some have passports and resources; others do not. Some are already targeted because of race, gender, faith, immigration status, or past record. Some have caregiving responsibilities, medical needs, or jobs that they cannot easily replace. Some live in places where a small act of defiance means a fine; others live where it can mean prison or worse.

Risk is not distributed evenly. Treating it as if it were turns movements into machines that grind down the very people they most need.

The question is not "How brave are you?" The question is "Given your real life, what risks can you take sustainably, and what protections do you need if you decide to take more?"

Low-Risk Actions That Still Matter

Low-risk does not mean low impact. It means actions that, for most people in your context, are unlikely to trigger severe retaliation. These are the things many can do consistently, often quietly, without blowing up their lives.

Examples include:

- Staying informed through trustworthy sources and sharing verified information, corrections, and context.
- Supporting independent media, legal funds, and civic organizations with small recurring donations.
- Having uncomfortable but calm conversations with friends, family, coworkers, or faith communities.
- Showing up at permitted demonstrations where risk of repression is relatively low.
- Signing petitions, contacting representatives, and participating in institutional channels that still function.

- Voting, observing elections, or volunteering in nonpartisan civic roles where that is still possible.
- Providing practical support, childcare, food, transport, for those taking more visible risks.

These actions rarely make headlines. They also rarely lead to arrests. What they do is stabilize the ground under everyone else: they keep information flowing, keep institutions under some pressure, and keep people who are on the front line from standing there alone.

If this is the lane you can occupy, you do not need to apologize for it. Done consistently, it matters.

Medium-Risk Actions: When You Need a Net

Medium-risk actions are those where consequences become more personal and less predictable. They may be legal but controversial, or technically allowed but likely to draw unwanted attention from employers, authorities, or hostile groups.

They can include:

- Organizing local groups, coalitions, or actions under your own name.
- Taking on visible roles in protests: marshaling, speaking, negotiating with authorities.
- Serving as a public spokesperson for a cause, online or offline.
- Joining or forming unions, associations, or internal caucuses that challenge powerful actors.
- Participating in sustained campaigns of disruption, boycotts, sit-ins, noncooperation, where some level of confrontation is expected.

- Doing sensitive documentation work: collecting testimony, filming abuses, tracking patterns.

These actions can be powerful. They can also bring real costs: job risk, harassment, doxxing, surveillance, or targeted legal pressure. They are not something one person should just "decide" to take on alone.

If you are moving into this lane, you need a net.

That means:

- People who know what you are doing and can check on you.
- Basic legal information and, where possible, contact with defense organizations before you need them.
- Agreements about what others will do if you face retaliation: statements of support, fundraising, practical help.
- Emotional support structures: friends, peers, or professionals who understand the stress you are under.

Medium-risk actions without support quickly turn into burnout and bitterness. With support, they can be sustained and shared.

HIGH-RISK ACTIONS: WHEN THEY MAKE SENSE AND WHEN THEY DON'T

High-risk actions are those where serious consequences are likely: arrest, assault, loss of livelihood, expulsion, long-term surveillance, or threats to you and your family. What counts as "high risk" varies by country and identity, but you usually know when you are crossing into this zone. Your body tells you.

These actions might include:

- Leading unauthorized or banned demonstrations in highly repressive environments.
- Publicly defying orders or laws in ways that carry known criminal penalties.
- Whistleblowing with sensitive internal information.
- Organizing strikes or boycotts in sectors where retaliation is swift and severe.
- Providing visible support to groups or individuals already under heavy state pressure.

Sometimes, high-risk actions are necessary. History is full of moments where people decided that the moral cost of staying safe was higher than the personal cost of stepping forward. Their choices opened space for others.

But high-risk actions are not always the right move, and they are never something movements should demand as a baseline. They should be used sparingly, strategically, and with clear eyes.

Before you step into this lane, questions worth asking include:

- What is the concrete goal of this risk?
- Is there any other way to achieve that goal at lower cost?
- Who else is affected if I face consequences, family, dependents, colleagues?
- What support is realistically available if things go badly?
- Am I choosing this because it is needed, or because I feel guilty for not doing more?

If a group glorifies sacrifice but cannot or will not protect those who take the hits, something is wrong. Heroic stories are often written on the backs of people who were, in practice, abandoned.

CHAPTER 6

Why Not Everyone Should Take the Same Risks

Movements are ecosystems. They need different species.

If everyone chose only low-risk actions, some openings would never be created. If everyone rushed into high-risk actions, movements would burn through their people faster than they can bring them in. The point is not to get everyone to the same level. It is to have a **healthy distribution**, where:

- Those who can take more risk do so with intention and support.
- Those who cannot, or choose not to, hold other vital roles without shame.
- No one is treated as more "pure" for being more exposed, or as less worthy for being less so.

Differences in risk are inevitable. What you can choose is whether those differences become a source of division or a source of strength.

It helps to say things out loud:

- "I am in a position where I can risk more; here is what I am willing to do."
- "I cannot risk arrest, but I can provide logistics, money, care, or skills."
- "I am not ready for public roles, but I can document, research, or support those who are."

Clarity reduces resentment. It also reduces the quiet, corrosive guilt that comes from pretending.

How Movements Fail When They Demand Martyrdom

Movements often romanticize martyrs: the people who lose their jobs, freedom, or lives and whose names become symbols. Remembering them matters. Building cultures that *expect* more martyrs rarely ends well.

When martyrdom becomes the unspoken standard, several things happen:

- People hide their limits until they break.
- Those with the least protection, poor, young, marginalized, end up taking the hardest hits.
- Burnout and trauma accumulate faster than new leadership can develop.
- Internal criticism is silenced, because questioning strategy sounds like disrespecting sacrifice.

Authoritarian systems do not have to destroy movements that treat everyone as expendable. Those movements will destroy themselves.

A healthier approach honors sacrifice **without** turning it into a demand. It treats people who take extreme risks as one part of a larger story, not as proof that everyone else is failing. It invests as much energy into healing, protection, and long-term support as it does into celebrating daring actions.

If a movement's stories are all about being willing to die, and almost none are about being willing to stay, rest, adapt, and age, something is off.

CHAPTER 6

Choosing Your Lane Now

You do not have to fix your lane forever. Life will change. Your capacity will change. The context will change. But it is useful, right now, to make a provisional choice.

You can ask yourself:

- Given my responsibilities and vulnerabilities, what is my **baseline lane**: low, medium, or high risk?
- Within that lane, what specific actions actually fit me, my skills, my temperament, my situation?
- What support do I need, and who do I need to talk to, before I move further?

You might decide: "For now, I am a low-risk person who focuses on information, donations, and conversation." Or: "For now, I can take medium risks in organizing and public speaking, as long as I have a support circle." Or: "At this point in my life, I am ready to take high risks on specific issues, but only if I am not doing it alone or in secret."

Whatever you choose, write it down. Treat it as a commitment to yourself, not a judgment. When guilt or panic comes, and it will, you can return to that commitment and remember: this is not about earning worth. It is about staying in the fight long enough to matter.

The next chapter will turn toward protection in a more direct way: how to build circles of care, legal and emotional, around the risks people actually take. If this chapter worked, you should feel less pressure to prove yourself, and more clarity about where you stand.

That clarity is not selfish. It is part of what keeps resistance human.

7

HOLDING THE LINE WHEN THINGS GET HARDER

Every serious attempt to defend something worth keeping eventually runs into the same wall: it gets harder.

At first, there is adrenaline. There are new ideas, new connections, a sense of waking up. Over time, there are also bills, deadlines, family crises, health scares, and the slow, grinding realization that the people causing harm are not going to stop just because you have seen through them. The system, whatever shape it takes where you live, will push back. It will try to exhaust you, isolate you, and make you doubt both yourself and everyone around you.

This chapter is about that stage.

It is not about how to win an argument. It is about how to stay a person while the fight goes on.

CHAPTER 7

The Quiet Weapons: Exhaustion, Fear, and Isolation

Authoritarian systems do not just use force and law. They use **time**.

They count on you getting tired. They count on outrage fading faster than their capacity to grind on. They count on your friends drifting away, your group splitting, your hope shrinking to the size of your own life.

They have several quiet weapons:

- **Exhaustion**: flooding the zone with crises and controversies until you feel you can't keep up.
- **Fear**: using visible examples of punishment to make the risk of action feel ever-present, even when you are not directly targeted.
- **Isolation**: subtly or directly discouraging spaces where people can compare notes and realize they are seeing the same things.

The goal is not only to stop you from acting. It is to convince you that acting is pointless, that no one else cares as much as you do, or that you are somehow broken for feeling this deeply.

Recognizing these tactics does not make them less painful. It does, however, protect you from turning them into stories about your own failure.

You are not weak for getting tired. You are living in a system that is designed to tire you out.

Burnout and Moral Injury: When It Hurts to Care

Burnout is not just "being busy." It is what happens when you are asked to care and act beyond your capacity, again and again, without enough support or sense of progress.

It shows up as:

- Emotional numbness where you used to feel sharp concern.
- Irritability toward people on "your side."
- Trouble concentrating on anything but the next urgent thing, or on nothing at all.
- A sense that nothing you do matters, even if you are objectively doing a lot.

Moral injury is a related wound. It happens when you witness or participate in things that clash with your deepest values and feel powerless to change them. That can mean watching injustice happen to others and being unable to stop it. It can also mean making compromises you once swore you never would, because the alternatives felt worse in the moment.

Both burnout and moral injury are common in long struggles. They do not mean you are failing. They mean the situation is asking more than any one person can carry.

If you do not acknowledge them, they tend to leak out sideways: into bitterness, infighting, cynicism, or sudden withdrawal. You might find yourself attacking allies, sabotaging projects, or numbing out in ways that leave you feeling worse afterward.

The first step in holding the line is to admit when you are hurt.

CHAPTER 7

Why Care Is Not Weakness

In hard times, it is tempting to armor up. Empathy feels like a liability. You may catch yourself thinking, "If I cared less, this would hurt less," and assume that the only way to survive is to toughen into something harder.

There is a difference between **numbing** and **grounding**.

Numbing is shutting down parts of yourself so you do not feel as much. It can get you through a day or a crisis, but over time it closes the very channels that keep you human: connection, curiosity, the ability to be moved. Numbing can look like relentless sarcasm, endless scrolling, substance use, or simply refusing to let anything in that might make you sad.

Grounding is staying connected to what you care about while also staying connected to your body, your limits, and your surroundings. It might look like:

- Letting yourself feel grief or anger and then doing something small and concrete.
- Taking breaks on purpose instead of collapsing by accident.
- Continuing to notice beauty, humor, and kindness even when they feel out of place.

Care is not weakness. It is your compass. Without it, strategy turns into cold technique, and victory, if it comes, starts to look like the thing you were fighting.

The challenge is not to care less. It is to care in ways that are sustainable and shared.

Practices for Staying Human Under Pressure

You do not need a perfect self-care routine. You need a handful of practices that help you return to yourself.

Some possibilities:

- **Rhythms, not streaks**: instead of promising you will meditate, write, or exercise every single day and then feeling like a failure when you don't, aim for a rhythm: "a couple of times a week," "most mornings," "after big actions." Rhythms bend; streaks break.
- **Tiny grounding rituals**: a walk around the block after difficult calls, a few deep breaths before opening the news, a habit of touching a nearby object to remind yourself "I am here, right now." Small things matter more than grand plans you never start.
- **Honest check-ins**: people you can text "I'm not okay today" without having to explain everything. The point is not to solve each other. It is to remember you are not alone.
- **Boundaries around doom-scrolling**: set times when you deliberately do not consume news or social media, even if it is just the hour before bed or the first hour after waking. There will always be more horror to see. You are allowed to look away sometimes.
- **Spaces where nothing is at stake**: a book, a game, a hobby, a show, a craft, a spiritual practice, anything that reminds you that your identity is larger than your role in the struggle.

You may feel guilty making space for this. That guilt is part of the design of systems that want you either burned out or absent. Rest is not desertion. It is maintenance.

How to Step Back Without Disappearing

There will be times when you need to step back. Health changes. Family situations change. The pressure becomes too much.

Stepping back is not the same as vanishing.

If you disappear silently, people who relied on you may feel abandoned. They may also repeat the pattern with others, because they have no better script. If you step back **on purpose**, you can both protect yourself and help the group adapt.

That looks like:

- Saying, "I need to reduce what I'm doing for a while," before you collapse.
- Being specific: "I can't organize events right now, but I can still edit, or donate, or show up occasionally."
- Handing off responsibilities where possible instead of letting them drop.
- Staying in some minimal form of contact so people know you are alive and can welcome you back if and when you're ready.

You are allowed to renegotiate your role. In fact, movements last longer when people do this openly instead of driving themselves to the edge and then quitting everything.

If someone else steps back, resist the urge to treat it as betrayal. Ask what they need. Thank them for what they have already given. Keep the door open.

Recognizing When the System Is Working on You

One of the most useful questions you can ask yourself in difficult moments is: "Is this feeling purely mine, or is the system leaning on it?"

When you notice:

- A sudden belief that everyone else is lazy, naive, or secretly against you.
- A powerful urge to attack people on your own side over minor differences.
- A sense that nothing is real unless it is posted, filmed, or applauded.
- An inner voice insisting that you must respond to *every* outrage or you are complicit.

Pause.

You do not have to trust every thought that presents itself. Some are reactions to real patterns of betrayal or injustice. Others are echoes of a structure that would love to see you burn your energy on infighting, perfectionism, or performative gestures that leave you emptier than before.

You can ask:

- "What am I actually trying to protect right now?"
- "Is there a smaller, more concrete action I could take instead of spiraling?"
- "Who could I check this perception with before I act on it?"

You will not always catch yourself in time. No one does. But even occasionally stepping out of the stream is a win.

Why Care and Protection Are Strategic, Not Extra

It is tempting to treat emotional support, legal defense, and mutual aid as "side projects," separate from the "real work." In practice, they are part of the real work.

Authoritarian systems do not just target leaders. They target families, jobs, mental health, and trust. If movements do not build their own forms of protection, they effectively subcontract that job to the very systems they are challenging.

Care is not only about kindness; it is about **capacity**. A group that burns through people faster than it can bring them in will eventually shrink or deform. A group that expects everyone to be endlessly available will end up led by those whose lives are least constrained, which may or may not be the voices that most need to be amplified.

When you protect each other, through legal funds, emotional support, shared childcare, housing, food, or simply attention, you are not being soft. You are building a structure that can hold more pressure.

Staying Long Enough to Matter

No single action or chapter changes a system. What does is accumulation: of truth, of pressure, of refusal, of care.

Holding the line when things get harder is not about becoming invulnerable. It is about accepting that you will be tired, scared, and sometimes discouraged, and deciding, in advance, how you will respond when those feelings arrive.

You can:

- Expect pushback instead of treating it as a sign you should have stayed quiet.
- Accept that you will need to rest and adjust lanes over time.
- Build and protect relationships that outlast any one campaign.
- Remember that staying human is not a luxury; it is the point.

If this chapter does what it is meant to do, you should not feel pressured to be endlessly strong. You should feel slightly more permission to be a person in the middle of all this, and to design your involvement so that you are still here later, when your calm, your memory, and your presence may matter even more than they do now.

8

WHAT HISTORY ACTUALLY SHOWS US ABOUT CHANGE

When the news feels like a slow-motion avalanche, it is easy to reach for two comforting lies. One says, "It will all work out somehow; history bends toward justice." The other says, "Nothing we do matters; power always wins." Both are ways of stepping back from responsibility. Both ignore what history actually shows.

This chapter is not a pep talk. It is a reality check, in both directions.

How Authoritarian Systems Really Fall

If you look across different countries and eras, a few patterns repeat when entrenched systems finally give way.

They rarely fall because one brave person makes the perfect speech or because one protest breaks through. They fall when **multiple pillars** that keep them standing, elites, security forces, bureaucrats, business interests, foreign backers, and the wider public, stop cooperating at the same time or close together.

Sometimes this happens gradually, through negotiated transitions. Sometimes it happens suddenly, through elections, mass protests, or internal splits. Often it is a mix: years of slow erosion behind the scenes, followed by what looks from the outside like an abrupt break.

The important point is that change usually comes when:

- Enough people **outside** the system have refused to normalize it, documented its harms, and built alternatives.
- Enough people **inside** the system start to calculate that staying loyal is riskier than stepping away.
- A trigger, a rigged election, a scandal, a failed crackdown, an economic shock, pushes those existing tensions past what the system can absorb.

In other words, systems fall not just because people resist, but because resistance interacts with internal weakness.

Why They Often Look Strongest Before They Fracture

Just before many regimes weaken, they look frighteningly solid.

You see:

- Huge rallies staged in their favor.
- New laws and crackdowns that make them seem untouchable.
- Propaganda insisting that resistance is tiny or crushed.

Part of this is projection. Parties and leaders who feel vulnerable often double down on displays of strength. They want to convince you that you are already defeated so that you stop doing the very things that scare them.

Part of it is structural. When systems feel pressure, they first use the tools they know best repression, co-optation, and spectacle, to reassert control. Sometimes it works. Sometimes it only pushes discontent underground, where it continues to accumulate. From the outside, you see the performance. From the inside, there may be cracks: quiet dissent in institutions, financial strain, exhaustion among loyalists, rising fear of what will happen *after* the current leaders are gone.

This is not a guarantee that "the worse it gets, the closer we are to victory." Sometimes it just gets worse. But it does mean that apparent strength is not the same as stability. Systems often look most monolithic right before we learn they were hollow in more places than anyone realized.

The Role of Patience and Timing

History is full of people who did the right thing at the wrong time and saw little immediate effect. It is also full of people who did something small at exactly the moment when conditions were ripe and watched it spread.

That does not mean you can predict the perfect moment. It does mean timing matters.

Patience in this context is not passive. It is the work of:

- **Keeping structures alive** organizations, relationships, skills, during long stretches when visible progress is minimal.

- **Building capacity** so that when windows open, you have people, plans, and networks ready.
- **Resisting the urge** to declare victory or defeat too early based on short-term swings.

Many of the "sudden" shifts we celebrate, a stunning election result, a rapid cascade of defections, a wave of protests, rest on years of groundwork that did not look like success while it was happening: community meetings with ten people, newsletters read by a few hundred, legal battles that seemed to go nowhere, friendships maintained across differences.

You cannot control timing. You can control whether the work you're doing now leaves future people more prepared or more alone.

Why People Underestimate Slow Wins

Our stories about change are biased toward drama. We remember the fall of a wall, the toppling of a statue, the day a law was signed or struck down. We forget the long chain of less visible wins that made those moments possible.

Slow wins look like:

- A generation of students raised with a more accurate understanding of rights and history.
- Local communities quietly building institutions that don't resemble the national dysfunction.
- Courts that, even in a skewed system, set precedents that later become tools.
- Dozens of small organizations learning, failing, and trying again until they find strategies that work in their context.

Slow wins also include things that **didn't happen** because people showed up: laws that were watered down, appointments that were blocked, abuses that stopped at one level and didn't spread further. These are hard to celebrate because they leave no dramatic before-and-after. Yet they change the trajectory.

When you only look for cinematic victories, you miss the reality that much of what protects people and creates futures is boring, repetitive, and cumulative. You might be living inside a slow win without recognizing it.

Why Collapse Rarely Looks Like a Movie

In films, bad systems fall with flourish. There is a clear climax. The villain is defeated. Crowds cheer. The screen fades to black.

In real life:

- Old elites often try to reinvent themselves inside the new order.
- New institutions inherit some habits of the old ones.
- Wounds, distrust, and inequalities persist.
- The people who did the hardest work may not be the ones who end up in charge.

Transitions are messy and uneven. Some things get better quickly; others take years. There are backlashes, disappointments, and half-measures.

This matters because if you expect a clean, cathartic ending, you will either:

- Declare defeat because reality does not match the movie in your head, or

- Declare victory too early, then be unprepared when old forces regroup.

History shows that even successful transitions require further defense and repair. The fall of one regime is the beginning of a new struggle over what replaces it, not the end of the story. That is not a reason for cynicism. It is a reason to see political time as longer than a news cycle.

Hope Without Lies

Hope is not the belief that things will work out no matter what. That belief is a luxury history does not support.

Hope, in this context, is something narrower and harder: the conviction that what you do still **changes the field**, even when you cannot see the whole board. It is the decision to act as if your efforts could matter, because when enough people make that decision, history tells us they often do.

What history actually shows is:

- Authoritarian systems are more fragile than they look, and more adaptable than we wish.
- People and institutions are capable of both surprising courage and disappointing compromise.
- No victory is pure, no defeat total.
- The difference between "nothing changed" and "everything changed" is often made of thousands of decisions by people who assumed they were small.

This chapter is not asking you to be optimistic. It is asking you to be accurate.

Accurate about the danger, so you do not drift back into denial.

CHAPTER 8

Accurate about the possibilities, so you do not collapse into despair.

What comes next in this book will turn from patterns back to you: how to carry this knowledge into the choices you make in your own context, what you support, what you refuse, and how you talk to the people around you, knowing that you are neither alone nor all-powerful, but still part of the story that will be told later about what happened here.

Chapter References:
Ackerman, B. (2014). *The Long Arc of Justice*. Harvard University Press.

Bueno de Mesquita, B., & Smith, A. (2011). *The Dictator's Handbook: Why bad behavior is almost always good politics*. PublicAffairs.

Chenoweth, E., & Stephan, M. J. (2011). *Why Civil Resistance Works: The strategic logic of nonviolent conflict*. Columbia University Press.

Levitsky, S., & Ziblatt, D. (2018). *How Democracies Die*. Crown.

O'Donnell, G., Schmitter, P. C., & Whitehead, L. (Eds.). (1986). *Transitions from Authoritarian Rule: Tentative conclusions about uncertain democracies*. Johns Hopkins University Press.

Tarrow, S. (1998). *Power in Movement: Social movements and contentious politics* (2nd ed.). Cambridge University Press.

9

IF YOU'RE STILL HERE, YOU'RE NOT ALONE

*I*f you are reading this far, something in you has refused to look away.

Maybe it is a quiet refusal. Maybe you have not marched or posted or joined anything. Maybe all you have done so far is notice, feel uneasy, and keep turning pages. That still counts. In a culture that keeps telling you to scroll past, to numb out, or to pick a side and stop thinking, staying present with discomfort is already an act.

By this point in the book you may be carrying two competing feelings at once. One is clarity. You see patterns more clearly than you did before. You can name what feels wrong without feeling quite as lost inside it. You know this moment is real. The other is uncertainty. A quieter, heavier question that does not always show up in words. Okay. Now what?

This chapter is not here to send you back out charged up and shaking. It is not a checklist, and it is not a recruitment pitch. It exists to help you stand on your own feet and stay human while this is unfolding.

CHAPTER 9

You Are Not Crazy

When institutions dim slowly, people who notice first often feel like the strange ones.

You see patterns others shrug off. You feel a tightness in your body when someone calls cruelty "just politics." You watch laws, norms, or news coverage shift and wonder why more people are not alarmed. At the same time, your daily life still mostly works. You can go to the store. You can attend school or work. There are jokes and meals and small pleasures. That mismatch between the ordinary surface of life and the slow-moving distortion underneath can make you doubt your own perception.

If part of you has been wondering, "Am I overreacting?", hear this plainly: it is not irrational to be unsettled by what you see. It is not paranoid to connect events instead of treating each one as an accident. It is not melodramatic to care about what happens beyond your own front door.

There is a name for the dynamic at work here. Researchers in political philosophy have begun using the concept of collective gaslighting to describe what happens when political systems systematically erode citizens' confidence in their own judgment. Natascha Rietdijk, a philosopher at Tilburg University, published a study in the Cambridge journal Episteme arguing that post-truth political rhetoric operates through the same mechanisms as interpersonal gaslighting: introducing competing narratives, discrediting critics, and denying observable facts, all with the cumulative effect of undermining what she calls epistemic self-trust, the basic belief that your cognitive faculties are reliable and that you are capable of forming accurate judgments about the world around you.

Political scientists Eric Beerbohm and Ryan Davis extended this analysis in the American Journal of Political Science, arguing that political gaslighting poses a distinctive threat to democracy because it targets the very capacity citizens need in order to participate: the confidence that what they see is real and that their assessment of it matters. The gaslighter does not merely lie. The gaslighter makes you doubt your ability to tell when someone is lying. That is why it feels so disorienting. It is designed to.

When many people, across different communities, professions, and political identities, begin asking the same uneasy questions at the same time, that is not hysteria. That is pattern recognition. And recognizing a pattern in the face of a system that is actively trying to make the pattern invisible is not weakness. It is the first requirement of staying free.

Could you sometimes misread a situation? Of course. Everyone does. But feeling the friction between what is said and what is done, between the story a country tells about itself and the way its institutions behave, is not a defect. It is a sign that your attention is still alive. Clarity does not require panic. It requires honesty.

Naming Fear Without Feeding It

Fear has been in the background of this entire book. Fear of what a government might do. Fear of what neighbors might accept. Fear of what it would cost you personally to take risks. Fear that the people you love will see this differently and that the distance will become permanent.

There is a persistent myth that courage looks like constant action, constant visibility, constant resolve. That myth burns people out and leaves only the most hardened voices standing. The truth is simpler and harder: fear will show up. Fatigue will show up. There may be moments when you go quiet, pull back, or choose rest over engagement. None of that disqualifies you. Human nervous systems were not designed for sustained high-alert living. Needing pauses does not mean you have abandoned your values. It means you are preserving your ability to live them over time.

There is no virtue in pretending you are not afraid. Fear is information. It tells you what you stand to lose. It tells you where you feel exposed. It reminds you that you are attached to people and futures that matter to you. What fear does not have to do is drive.

Where Fear Sits
The same emotion, three positions, three outcomes.

FEAR IS DRIVING	FEAR IS A PASSENGER	FEAR IS LOCKED AWAY
What it looks like:	**What it looks like:**	**What it looks like:**
Panic or paralysis	Acknowledged but not obeyed	Denied or suppressed
Reactive decisions	Deliberate choices	Numbness mistaken for strength
All-or-nothing thinking	Honest about limits	Reckless exposure
"Everything must happen NOW"	"I see the risk. I choose my route."	"I'm fine. Nothing bothers me."
What it produces:	**What it produces:**	**What it produces:**
Burnout within weeks	Sustained engagement	Sudden collapse
Broken relationships	Calibrated risk-taking	Disconnection from others
Energy spent without direction	Capacity preserved over time	Harm absorbed silently
Serves the system it opposes	Models courage for others	Others cannot assess real risk
▼	▼	▼
Exhaustion	Endurance	Fragility

Courage is not the absence of fear. It is the decision to keep a hand on the wheel.

When fear is behind the wheel, it tends to slam between two bad routes: paralysis and panic. Paralysis says, "There is nothing to be done; better not think about it." Panic says, "Everything must be done right now, no matter the cost." Both end up serving the same systems, because they burn your energy without building anything. When fear is locked in the trunk, denied or suppressed, it does not disappear. It accumulates. People who refuse to acknowledge fear often behave recklessly, take risks they have not assessed, and collapse suddenly rather than gradually. Others around them cannot gauge the real level of danger, because the person who should be feeling it is performing numbness instead.

The middle position is the one that lasts. Let fear ride in the passenger seat. Acknowledge it. Listen to what it points out. Then choose your route anyway, using the maps you have seen in these pages: the phases of erosion, the ways people can apply pressure, the lanes of risk that fit who you are and where you live. Courage here is not the absence of fear. It is the decision to keep a hand on the wheel. Participation is not a test you pass or fail. It is something you return to in different ways, in different seasons, according to your capacity. Staying human means refusing the lie that you must either sacrifice yourself entirely or step aside forever. There is a wide, necessary middle ground.

Dignity Is a Starting Point, Not a Reward

Authoritarian projects work hard to convince you that your worth depends on your usefulness: as a loyal supporter, as a "real" member of some identity group, as someone who never questions the story you are given. They also sometimes convince movements against them that worth must be earned in the opposite way: by taking the highest risks, having the purest opinions, or being endlessly available.

Both stories erase dignity.

Your dignity does not come from what you produce or how loudly you protest. It is not canceled by confusion, fatigue, or mistakes. It does not disappear because you are scared, or because there were months or years when you tried not to think about any of this.

Starting from dignity matters for a simple reason: people who believe they are worthless are easier to rule and easier to use. They are also more likely to lash out in ways that mirror the harm they have experienced. Knowing that you are already enough, before you sign up, before you donate, before you say anything out loud, is what allows your choices to be free, not driven by shame.

Resilience researchers have confirmed this intuition empirically. Catherine Panter-Brick, whose work at Yale on resilience across conflict zones was published in the European Journal of Psychotraumatology, found that resilience in its deepest form is not about "functioning well" or performing better than expected. It is about "making sense of the moral aspects of your life." In studies of families in Afghanistan, the factor that most reliably predicted long-term resilience was not material resources or even physical safety. It was the sustained sense of hope and dignity. People who could locate meaning in their actions, even small ones, even imperfect ones, maintained their capacity to act over time. People who could not, regardless of how strong they appeared, eventually hollowed out.

You do not have to earn the right to care about your own future. Dignity does not require victory. It requires consistency.

You Do Not Have to Convince Everyone You Love

A quiet fear many readers carry is not about institutions or politics at all. It is about relationships.

What if someone I love sees this differently? What if they think I have gone too far? What if staying connected requires staying silent?

There is no universal answer here, and anyone who pretends otherwise is selling certainty they do not possess.

What matters is this distinction: staying in relationship does not require surrendering your grip on reality, and holding your ground does not require contempt. Some conversations are worth having slowly, gently, with patience and care. Others will not move no matter how carefully you approach them. Learning the difference is part of staying sane.

You are allowed to set boundaries around what you will debate, what you will tolerate, and what you will no longer pretend is normal. You are allowed to step back from arguments that drain you without producing understanding. You are allowed to choose peace without choosing denial.

This is one of the places where the gaslighting research becomes personal rather than political. Rietdijk's work notes that gaslighting disproportionately affects people in relationships characterized by power asymmetries and emotional dependency. In families where political identity has become fused with personal loyalty, disagreement can feel not just uncomfortable but dangerous, as though questioning a policy is the same as rejecting a person. That conflation is itself a product of the polarization the playbook cultivates. It is not natural. It is manufactured. And recognizing that does not make the pain of navigating it any less real, but it can help you stop blaming yourself for a tension you did not create.

Connection that depends on your silence is not true connection. And separation that preserves your integrity is not failure.

How to Stay Oriented Without Drowning

Many people sense that something is wrong, yet feel overwhelmed by information itself. The news feels relentless. Social media feels distorted. Silence feels irresponsible. The result is a kind of epistemic vertigo: the feeling that the ground is always shifting and that any attempt to stand still will leave you behind.

Orientation does not come from consuming more. It comes from consuming intentionally. You do not need to know everything to know enough. You do not need to react to every development to remain engaged. You are allowed to curate what enters your mind without turning away from reality. Staying informed is not the same as staying inflamed. Wisdom often looks quieter than outrage.

These four questions are not a system. They are a reset. When you feel the ground moving, when a headline makes your chest tighten, when you have spent an hour scrolling and feel worse than when you started, stop and return to these. They will not answer every question. But they will tell you where you stand right now, and that is usually enough to take the next step.

A grounded posture also involves some practical disciplines. You value accuracy more than speed. You pause before sharing. You accept uncertainty when facts are still unfolding. You notice when information is designed to provoke rather than inform. You set limits around how much news you consume in a sitting, not because you do not care, but because you are protecting the part of yourself that does.

Connection and Responsibility

If you have ever felt like the only one noticing a pattern, it may help to remember how many other people are quietly thinking the same thing. Most will never write a book, give a speech, or lead a march. Many will never tell you what is in their head. But you are not the only person awake.

The real question is not "Am I alone?" It is "Where can I connect what I see with what someone else is already doing?"

Connection does not have to be dramatic. It can be a small local group where you can speak frankly without being told you are overreacting. A colleague who shares your unease about a policy and is willing to ask questions with you. A friend who will read the same article or chapter and talk about it over coffee. A community, faith, or professional space where you can gently widen the conversation.

Responsibility grows out of those connections. It is very hard to hold on to a sense of obligation to "the public" in the abstract. It is much easier to remember your responsibility when you can picture actual faces, people who will be affected by what you support, what you resist, and what you let slide. Responsibility here does not mean carrying everything. It means accepting that your choices are part of a web that extends beyond your own life. That is weighty. It is also what makes your life matter beyond the private circle of your own concerns.

Success Is Not Always Loud

One of the most damaging assumptions of our time is that if change is not dramatic, it is not real. History does not work that way.

Much of what protects societies does not announce itself. Harm prevented rarely makes headlines. Norms held quietly often matter more than battles won loudly. You may never know the full impact of the lines you hold. That does not make them insignificant. The work of preservation is often invisible until it fails. Choosing to protect what still exists is not less noble than trying to build something new.

When you only look for cinematic victories, you miss the reality that much of what protects people and creates futures is boring, repetitive, and cumulative. A generation of students raised with a more accurate understanding of rights and history. Local communities quietly building institutions that do not resemble the national dysfunction. Courts that, even in a skewed system, set precedents that later become tools. Dozens of small organizations learning, failing, and trying again until they find strategies that work in their context. These are slow wins. You might be living inside one without recognizing it.

Slow wins also include things that did not happen because people showed up: laws that were watered down, appointments that were blocked, abuses that stopped at one level and did not spread further. These are hard to celebrate because they leave no dramatic before-and-after. Yet they change the trajectory.

Where Meaning Comes From When Outcomes Are Uncertain

At some point, honest people stop asking, "Will this work?" and start asking, "How do I want to live while this is happening?"

That shift matters.

There is a difference between hope as prediction and hope as practice. One depends on outcomes you cannot control. The other depends on choices you can. Hope as prediction collapses the moment the news gets bad enough. Hope as practice survives because it was never anchored to a forecast. It was anchored to coherence: the knowledge that your actions align with your values, even when the future is unclear. The knowledge that if this moment is later explained to children, students, or strangers, your behavior will make sense.

Viktor Frankl, writing from the experience of surviving Nazi concentration camps, argued that the people who endured were not necessarily the strongest or the most optimistic. They were the ones who could locate meaning in their circumstances, however dire. Frankl was not offering a comfortable platitude. He was describing a psychological mechanism. The human capacity for meaning-making is not a luxury that arrives after safety. It is a survival tool that operates during danger. When meaning is present, people can tolerate extraordinary strain. When it is absent, even moderate pressure can cause collapse.

You do not need a grand theory of meaning. You need a thread of coherence between what you believe and how you behave. That thread is what holds identity together under pressure. It is also what others recognize when they are looking for someone to trust.

You Are Not Late

Some readers worry they are waking up too slowly. That they should have seen this sooner. That others are braver, faster, better informed. That is another lie, and it is a particularly effective one because it converts awareness into guilt and guilt into paralysis.

Awareness unfolds at different speeds because lives are different. Responsibilities are different. Risks are different. Some people had the luxury of paying attention early. Others were consumed by survival, caregiving, health, grief, or the simple demands of keeping a life together. The moment does not require everyone to arrive at once to be real. What matters is not when you noticed, but what you choose now that you have.

There is also a practical reason to reject the "too late" story. Movements that have changed the course of history consistently absorbed people at different stages. The Montgomery bus boycott lasted 381 days. Some people joined on day one. Some joined on day two hundred. The people who showed up late did not diminish the effort. They sustained it past the point where the people who showed up early were exhausted.

If you are arriving now, you are not late. You are reinforcement.

CHAPTER 9

Choosing One Small Next Thing

This book has covered a lot: phases of erosion, tactics of resistance, ways to use anger, different lanes of risk, how to stay oriented, how to tell when a group is healthy and when it is not. It is not meant to be implemented all at once. If you try, you will likely end up doing nothing.

Instead, treat it like a toolbox you visit as needed. Right now, at this point in the book, the practical question is small: what is one next thing that fits who you are, where you are, and what you can honestly risk?

It might be paying closer attention to a specific institution you are part of and noticing when its behavior shifts. It might be joining a local effort you have been watching from a distance, even if all you do at first is listen. It might be writing or speaking carefully about one pattern that keeps bothering you. It might be setting a boundary around how much time you spend absorbing news without acting. It might be offering support, material, emotional, or logistical, to someone else whose lane is more exposed than yours. It might be having one honest conversation with someone you have been avoiding.

None of these actions will, by themselves, stop a slide toward authoritarianism or repair what has already been damaged. But they move you from spectator to participant. They align your inner unease with outer behavior. They make you a little harder to manage and a little easier to find. That is how change always begins: with many people, in many places, deciding to be slightly more honest and slightly more connected than they were before.

IF YOU ARE STILL HERE

If you are still here, you have already done something systems of control try desperately to prevent: you have stayed with a difficult subject long enough to see its shape.

You are not being asked to become a hero. You are being invited to stay human: curious, limited, capable of learning, capable of refusing, capable of starting again after you are tired.

You are not being told that everything will work out. You are being told that what you do still matters, and that there are others, many of them invisible to you, who are also trying in their own ways to hold a line.

You are not crazy for seeing what you see. You are not alone in fearing what you fear. You are not powerless, even if you are not in charge. You are not late, even if you wish you had started sooner.

You have choices. How you use your anger. How you talk. What you normalize. What you refuse. Where you place your time, your money, your attention, your care. None of these choices will save the world alone. Together, they shape the ground on which everyone else stands.

If this book has done its job, you should feel neither safe in denial nor stranded in despair. You should feel a little more oriented: aware of the risks, aware of the tools, aware that your dignity and your capacity to connect with others are still intact.

From here, there is no script. There is only the ongoing work of staying awake, staying kind, and doing what you can with the life you have, alongside others who are trying to do the same.

If you are still here, you are not alone.

CHAPTER 9

Chapter References:

Beerbohm, E., & Davis, R. (2023). Gaslighting citizens. American Journal of Political Science, 67(1), 165-180.

Chenoweth, E., & Stephan, M. J. (2011). Why civil resistance works: The strategic logic of nonviolent conflict. Columbia University Press.

Frankl, V. E. (1946/2006). Man's search for meaning. Beacon Press.

Masten, A. S. (2001). Ordinary magic: Resilience processes in development. American Psychologist, 56(3), 227-238.

Merriam-Webster. (2022). Word of the year 2022: Gaslighting. https://www.merriam-webster.com/wordplay/word-of-the-year

Panter-Brick, C., & Eggerman, M. (2012). Understanding culture, resilience, and mental health: The production of hope. In M. Ungar (Ed.), The social ecology of resilience (pp. 369-386). Springer.

Panter-Brick, C., & Leckman, J. F. (2013). Editorial commentary: Resilience in child development. Journal of Child Psychology and Psychiatry, 54(4), 333-336.

Rietdijk, N. (2021). Post-truth politics and collective gaslighting. Episteme, 18(4), 637-651. Cambridge University Press.

Southwick, S. M., Bonanno, G. A., Masten, A. S., Panter-Brick, C., & Yehuda, R. (2014). Resilience definitions, theory, and challenges: Interdisciplinary perspectives. European Journal of Psychotraumatology, 5(1), 25338.

Stern, R. (2007). The gaslight effect: How to spot and survive the hidden manipulation others use to control your life. Harmony Books.

Werner, E. E., & Smith, R. S. (1992). Overcoming the odds: High risk children from birth to adulthood. Cornell University Press.

10

WHAT WE BUILD

WHEN THE ANGER BECOME A BLUEPRINT

*T*hroughout this book, we have talked about what is broken. We have named the anger. We have explored who benefits from division and why. We have looked at the playbooks used to keep people afraid, confused, and fighting each other instead of the systems that are failing them.

This chapter is about what we do next.

Not in theory. Not as a slogan. Not as another protest movement or think tank white paper that sits on a shelf while the country continues to fracture. This is about the concrete, structural frameworks that already exist for rebuilding the way we choose, train, and hold accountable the people we send to govern on our behalf. Some of these frameworks are well-tested. Some are emerging. None of them alone is sufficient. Together, they represent the most serious effort in a generation to repair a democracy that has been systematically rigged against the people it claims to serve.

CHAPTER 10

The Problem Is Not You

Let me say something directly: you should not need a PhD in political science to be an informed voter. You should not need to decode campaign finance filings or cross-reference legislative voting records against donor lists just to figure out whether the person on your ballot is going to serve you or sell you out. That is not a functioning democracy. That is a rigged system wearing the costume of one.

The problem is not that Americans are too dumb or too lazy to participate. The problem is that the system was designed, over decades, to make participation feel pointless. Gerrymandered districts that predetermine outcomes. Primary elections dominated by extreme base voters because moderates stay home. Politicians who enter office middle-class and leave as millionaires. Insider trading protections that apply to Congress but not to the rest of us. A revolving door between Capitol Hill and lobbying firms so well-oiled it barely squeaks anymore.

Voters did not create this mess. The people in power did. And then they told you it was your fault for not showing up.

The good news, and it is genuinely good news, is that across the country, people have stopped waiting for Congress to fix itself. They are building the tools to fix it from the outside, city by city, state by state, framework by framework. What follows is a map of those tools. Not a sales pitch for any one of them. A landscape.

The Reform Landscape

There is no single reform that will repair American democracy. Anyone who tells you otherwise is either simplifying for effect or selling something. The damage is structural, layered, and self-reinforcing. Gerrymandering protects incumbents who block campaign finance reform, which ensures that the donor class controls who runs, which ensures that the people who draw district lines remain in power. Each broken piece supports the others. That means the fix also has to be layered.

The Reform Landscape
Different entry points. Same broken machine.

	WHAT IT FIXES	HOW IT WORKS	TRACK RECORD	LIMITATIONS
ANTI-CORRUPTION ACTS	Lobbying, dark money, ethics loopholes, revolving door	Model legislation passed city by city, state by state	197 laws passed across multiple states as of 2025	Slow. Varies by state. Requires ballot initiative access
RANKED CHOICE VOTING	Spoiler effect, lesser-of-two-evils, negative campaigning	Voters rank candidates; winner needs true majority	Used in 52 cities, 2 states. NYC adopted 2021	Banned in 17 states. Voter confusion claims (disputed)
OPEN PRIMARIES	Extreme candidates chosen by small partisan base	All candidates, one ballot; top finishers advance regardless	California, Alaska, Washington, Nebraska use variations	Both parties resist. Mixed evidence on moderation
INDEPENDENT REDISTRICTING	Gerrymandering; politicians choosing their voters	Citizen commissions draw district lines instead of legislators	14 states use independent or bipartisan models	Only helps at next census. Vulnerable to court challenges
VALUES CONTRACTS	Broken promises; no accountability after election	Candidates sign enforceable pledges before running	Emerging model. Bridge Party Pact is one framework	Untested at scale. Enforcement is the open question
SMALL-DOLLAR PUBLIC FUNDING	Donor class controls who can afford to run for office	Vouchers or matching funds amplify small donations	Seattle voucher program. NYC matching funds	Costs money. Taxpayer funding of campaigns is divisive

No single reform fixes the system. They work together.
Anti-corruption laws close loopholes. Electoral reforms change incentives.

The question is not which reform is best.
The question is which entry point fits your community, your state, and your capacity.

Each of these reforms attacks a different part of the machine. Anti-corruption acts close the legal loopholes that allow politicians to take money from the interests that lobby them. Ranked choice voting changes the incentive structure of elections so that candidates benefit from broad appeal rather than extreme positioning.

Open primaries break the stranglehold that small partisan bases have over who appears on the general election ballot. Independent redistricting commissions take the power to draw district lines away from the politicians who benefit from rigging them. Values contracts create enforceable accountability mechanisms that go beyond campaign promises. Small-dollar public funding changes who can afford to run for office in the first place.

No single entry point is the right one for every community, every state, or every citizen. The question is not which reform is best. The question is which entry point fits where you live, what is politically viable in your context, and what you are positioned to support.

Anti-Corruption: The Foundation Layer

If there is a place to start, it is corruption. Not because it is the most dramatic reform, but because it is the one that makes every other reform possible.

RepresentUs, the largest nonpartisan anti-corruption organization in the country, has spent more than a decade advancing a piece of model legislation called the American Anti-Corruption Act. The Act was crafted by former Federal Election Commission chairman Trevor Potter in consultation with constitutional attorneys across the political spectrum, and its provisions are designed to survive court challenges. It targets the specific mechanisms by which money distorts governance: it makes it illegal for politicians to take money from the lobbyists who lobby them, bans lobbyist bundling, closes the revolving door between Congress and K Street, and requires full transparency in political spending.

What makes RepresentUs notable is not the legislation itself but the strategy behind it. The organization concluded early on that going through Congress was futile, because the people who would need to pass the reforms are the same people who benefit from the current system. So it went around Congress entirely. It focused on ballot initiatives, working city by city and state by state to pass local and state-level anti-corruption laws. As of 2025, the movement has helped pass 197 anti-corruption and pro-democracy laws across the country. In 2024 alone, voters in Maine approved a measure to limit super PAC contributions, voters in Los Angeles created an independent redistricting commission, Richmond and Washington, D.C. adopted ranked choice voting, and Arizona voters defeated four separate attempts to rewrite the state constitution.

The theory of change is cumulative. RepresentUs estimates that if roughly 3.5 percent of the population, around eleven million Americans, becomes actively engaged in anti-corruption reform, systemic change becomes inevitable. That number is not arbitrary. It draws on research into the critical mass required for social movements to shift group norms and institutional behavior. Below the threshold, reform movements stall. Above it, the shift becomes self-reinforcing.

Electoral Reform: Changing the Incentives

Corruption is the disease. But the electoral system is the delivery mechanism.

Consider how American elections currently work. In most states, primary elections are closed to registered party members, which means a small, ideologically committed fraction of voters determines which candidates appear on the general election ballot. In safe districts, the primary is the real election, and the incentive for candidates is to appeal to the most extreme voices in their base rather than to the broader public. Gerrymandered maps ensure that most districts are safe, which means most members of Congress face more danger from a primary challenge within their own party than from the opposing party. The entire system selects for extremism and punishes moderation.

Ranked choice voting addresses part of this by changing how winners are determined. Instead of plurality wins, where a candidate can win with less than a majority, RCV requires candidates to build broad coalitions. Voters rank candidates in order of preference, and if no one wins a majority of first-choice votes, the lowest-performing candidate is eliminated and their voters' second choices are redistributed. The process repeats until someone crosses the majority threshold. Research published through the American Bar Association's 2025 update on RCV found that the system reduces negative campaigning, because candidates need to be acceptable as a second or third choice to voters whose first choice may be a rival. It also reduces the spoiler effect that has historically crushed third-party and independent candidates.

As of 2025, ranked choice voting is used in 52 jurisdictions across 23 states, including statewide in Alaska and Maine. New York City adopted it for most city elections in 2021. In the 2025 Democratic mayoral primary, the system produced a winner who built a genuinely broad coalition across the city's diverse boroughs. Two-thirds of Americans, when surveyed, favor comprehensive election reform, and younger voters are significantly more supportive of alternative voting systems than older generations.

The resistance is real. Seventeen states have banned RCV outright, and both major parties have reasons to oppose reforms that reduce their gatekeeping power. But the trajectory is clear: where voters have experienced the system, satisfaction is high, and repeal efforts have consistently failed. Alaska, Georgia, Utah, and Bloomington,

Minnesota all voted to keep their RCV systems in 2024 after organized efforts to reverse them.

Open primaries attack the problem from a different angle. California's top-two primary, Alaska's top-four system, and similar models in Washington and Nebraska allow all voters to participate in a single primary regardless of party registration, with the top finishers advancing to the general election. The effect is to break the chokehold that small partisan bases have over candidate selection. When a broader electorate participates in the primary, candidates who can speak across ideological lines have a structural advantage. The National Association of Nonpartisan Reformers, a coalition of dozens of organizations including FairVote, the Independent Voter Project, and the Bridge Alliance, coordinates strategy across these overlapping reform efforts.

Values Contracts: The Emerging Model

Anti-corruption laws change what politicians are allowed to do. Electoral reforms change the incentives they face. But there is a third layer that neither of those fully addresses: what happens after someone takes office and discovers that the easiest path is still the path of least resistance?

This is the gap that values contract frameworks are designed to fill. The idea is straightforward: before a candidate receives endorsement, training, or financial support, they sign a legally binding public agreement committing to specific ethical standards that go far beyond what the law requires. If they violate the contract, they are publicly removed, the violation is announced, and legal action is pursued to reclaim resources.

The Bridge Party Pact is one such framework, and it is the one I have been involved in developing. I am transparent about that. But the concept of enforceable values contracts is not limited to a single organization, and the principle matters more than any particular vehicle. What matters is the mechanism: a system in which a candidate's word is not just a campaign promise but a contractual obligation with real consequences.

The BPP is built on 12 core values: integrity, compassion, courage, humility, wisdom, justice, unity, accountability, truthfulness, stewardship, innovation, and empathy. These are not bumper stickers. They are the basis of a contract that requires every decision a BPP-endorsed candidate makes to be explicitly tied to one or more of those values. The contract includes transparency requirements far beyond current law: annual public tax returns, quarterly financial disclosures, a complete ban on individual stock trading while in office, public logs of all gifts, meetings, and campaign travel, and an anti-blackmail provision called the Integrity Ledger, in which candidates proactively disclose potential vulnerabilities so they cannot be leveraged through fear and secrets.

The BPP is not a third party. It does not ask anyone to leave the Democratic Party or the Republican Party. That approach has been tried repeatedly and it has failed repeatedly, from the Reform Party to Americans Elect to the Forward Party. The BPP plants itself inside both parties simultaneously, creating BPP-aligned candidates who are bound by the same contract and accountable to the same standards regardless of which side of the aisle they sit on. Research from the University of Pennsylvania has established that when a committed minority reaches roughly 25 percent of a population, systemic change becomes not just possible but unstoppable. The BPP does not need a majority. It needs enough principled leaders in both parties to form a swing coalition that forces bipartisan governance as the price of getting anything done.

The values in the contract are not liberal or conservative. Integrity is not a partisan position. Compassion does not belong to the left.

Accountability does not belong to the right. When the BPP presents its core values to different audiences, the framing adapts but the commitment does not. For BPP Democrats, human dignity means every person deserves respect, opportunity, and protection of rights. For BPP Republicans, it means every person is made in God's image and deserves dignity. The value is identical. The language is adapted. The policy commitment is the same.

The enforcement mechanism is what distinguishes a values contract from a traditional campaign pledge. A traditional promise has no consequences when broken. A BPP contract has public removal, financial reclamation, and an independent ethics process. The contract does not assume good faith. It assumes politicians are human, and it builds accountability around that assumption.

What This Kind of Leader Looks Like

A note before this section: this book does not endorse candidates. It does not tell you who to vote for. What it does is describe a set of qualities that the research, the history, and the patterns laid out in these pages suggest are essential for leaders who want to repair rather than exploit a damaged democracy. What follows is a case study in those qualities, not a recommendation on any ballot.

James Talarico is a Democratic state representative from Texas who has never taken corporate PAC money in his entire legislative career. He is the only member of the Texas Legislature who can make that claim. He is a former public school teacher who taught sixth-grade English in one of the poorest zip codes in San Antonio through Teach For America before entering politics. He later earned a master's degree from Harvard's Graduate School of Education. When he was diagnosed with Type 1 diabetes during his first campaign, after nearly collapsing while walking 25 miles across his district, he turned that personal crisis into legislative action and helped pass a bill capping insulin costs at 25 dollars a month in Texas.

What makes Talarico a useful case study for this chapter is not his party affiliation. It is the structural alignment between how he operates and the principles this book has laid out.

First, he leads from values rather than positioning. Talarico is a Presbyterian seminarian whose grandfather was a Baptist preacher in South Texas. His political identity is explicitly rooted in a moral framework rather than an ideological one. He frames politics not as left versus right but as a question of whether the powerful serve or exploit the people they govern. He has called Christian nationalism a cancer on Christianity and has gone viral for calmly dismantling colleagues who attempt to use Scripture to justify policies that harm the poor, the sick, and the marginalized. Whether you share his theological commitments or not, the structure is what matters: he can explain why he holds every position he holds, and the explanation traces back to a coherent set of principles rather than to polling data or donor preferences.

Second, he has demonstrated the capacity to reach across the boundaries that the partisan system creates. Talarico flipped a Texas state House district that had not backed a Democratic presidential candidate since Jimmy Carter. He did not do it by disguising his views. He did it by speaking in a register that people across the political spectrum could hear. When he appeared on The Joe Rogan Experience in 2025, a platform whose audience skews conservative, the host told him at the end of the conversation that he should run for president. That response did not come because Talarico told Rogan what he wanted to hear. It came because Talarico was consistent. He tied every position to a clear moral framework, and consistency, as this book has argued from the beginning, is what people are starving for in an era of manufactured incoherence.

Third, his funding model demonstrates that the donor-class dependency is a choice, not a necessity. When Talarico announced his candidacy for the United States Senate, he raised nearly seven million dollars in three weeks, overwhelmingly from small-dollar donations from working people across nearly every county in Texas. That is not a fluke. It is evidence that when a candidate offers coherence and accountability, the fundraising model that the political establishment insists is impossible becomes not only possible but powerful.

Talarico is not a BPP candidate. He did not emerge from any of the reform frameworks described in this chapter. That is precisely the point. He is proof that the kind of leader these frameworks are designed to find, train, and support already exists in the wild. The question is not whether such people exist. The question is whether we can build systems that produce hundreds more of them, across both parties, bound by shared standards of transparency and accountability rather than by the loyalty demands of the donor class and the party machinery.

The patterns this book has described, the erosion, the playbooks, the normalization, the gaslighting, are not abstractions. They are the environment in which real people must decide whether to enter public life and on what terms. Leaders who can see those patterns, name them honestly, and still choose to engage without becoming what they oppose are not mythological figures. They are the minimum standard a functioning democracy requires. The reform frameworks in this chapter exist to make that standard the rule rather than the exception.

Why Reform Must Cross Party Lines

Some people will read this chapter and think: this sounds like it belongs in one party more than the other. That reaction is itself a symptom of the problem.

Both parties have members who trade stocks on insider information. Both parties have leaders beholden to mega-donors. Both parties punish members who reach across the aisle. Both parties have lost the trust of the American people, with approval ratings in the basement and a full 32 percent of voters now refusing to affiliate with either one. The entire premise of American polarization depends on convincing you that the other side has a monopoly on bad faith. The data says otherwise.

Every reform framework described in this chapter works better when it crosses party lines. Anti-corruption laws passed by ballot initiative succeed precisely because they bypass partisan legislatures and go directly to voters, who support them regardless of party. Ranked choice voting reduces polarization because it rewards candidates who can appeal beyond their base. Values contracts work inside both parties simultaneously because they create a shared standard that makes partisan identity secondary to ethical accountability.

If you only reform one side, the other side exploits the gap. But if you build systems that hold everyone to the same standard, regardless of which side of the aisle they sit on, you create something that has never existed in modern American politics: a functional coalition of conscience inside the system, not trying to replace it.

The Objections You Are Already Thinking

These reforms are naive. Every structural reform in American history was called naive before it worked. Women's suffrage was naive. The Civil Rights Act was naive. Marriage equality was naive. The pattern is consistent: the people who benefit from the current system declare alternatives impossible until the alternatives succeed, at which point they are rebranded as inevitable. RepresentUs alone has helped pass 197 laws that were called naive before they were on the books.

Politicians will just sign values contracts and break them. Some will try. That is why enforcement mechanisms exist. A traditional campaign promise has no consequences when broken. A values contract has public removal, financial reclamation, and an independent ethics process. The contract does not assume good faith. It assumes that politicians are human and builds accountability around that assumption.

The parties will crush this. They will try. Party leadership will call reform-aligned members disloyal. They may deny them committee assignments or fund primary challengers against them. Every such attack becomes evidence of the problem the reforms were created to solve. When an incumbent retaliates against a colleague for refusing corporate PAC money, the retaliation tells voters more about the system than any position paper could.

This is just centrism with extra steps. No. Centrism says meet in the middle on everything. These reforms say some things are not negotiable: honesty, transparency, service over self-interest, accountability to voters rather than donors. Those are not moderate positions. Those are moral positions. None of these frameworks ask anyone to split the difference between right and wrong. They ask leaders to anchor every decision in a shared set of principles and to prove the connection publicly.

Where is the money going to come from? From the same place it came from in every successful reform movement: from ordinary people who are tired of being sold out and are willing to invest in something different. Talarico raised seven million dollars in three weeks from small donors. RepresentUs raised enough to pass laws in dozens of states. Seattle funds its democracy voucher program through a modest property tax increase. The money exists. What has been missing is a credible vehicle for it.

CHAPTER 10

What Changes When This Works

Imagine a state where anti-corruption laws have closed the revolving door, ranked choice voting has changed the incentive structure, open primaries have broken the base voter stranglehold, and a handful of values-contract candidates hold the swing votes in the legislature. The majority party cannot pass extreme legislation on party lines because reform-aligned members will not vote for anything that violates their contract, even if their leadership demands it. The minority party cannot simply obstruct because reform-aligned members on their side are committed to finding common ground. The reform caucus becomes a swing vote that forces every bill through a filter of shared principles. The result is not paralysis. It is governance.

Imagine a congressional race where a reform-aligned candidate campaigns on total financial transparency, no stock trading, no corporate PAC money, and quarterly town halls. Their opponent, a career politician backed by millions in dark money, has to explain why they will not sign the same contract. The mere existence of a reform candidate in the race raises the standard for everyone. Even candidates who have no connection to any reform framework will feel pressure to match its transparency commitments because voters will start asking why they will not.

Imagine a generation of voters who grew up seeing politicians held to enforceable ethical standards. Young people who saw that corruption was named and punished rather than tolerated and excused. Imagine those young people deciding to run for office themselves, not because they wanted power but because they saw a system that actually rewarded service.

That is what changes. Not overnight. Not in one election cycle. But steadily, reform by reform, law by law, leader by leader.

What You Can Do Right Now

You do not have to run for office to be part of this. Every framework described in this chapter is designed to function at multiple levels of engagement.

You can support anti-corruption ballot initiatives in your state. RepresentUs maintains a map of active campaigns and local chapters. You can advocate for ranked choice voting or open primaries in your city or county. FairVote, the Campaign Legal Center, and the National Association of Nonpartisan Reformers all provide toolkits for local organizers. You can sign the Bridge Party Pact as a voter, a public commitment to support candidates who meet the BPP standard regardless of party. You can start a local Bridge Team, a group from your community that identifies potential reform-aligned candidates and supports them. You can host a conversation where people from different parties sit down together and discover that they agree on far more than the system wants them to believe.

You can also do something simpler and more immediate. Look at the candidates on your ballot right now and ask three questions. Do they take corporate PAC money? Will they release their tax returns? Will they commit to not trading individual stocks while in office? If the answer to any of those is no, ask yourself why you are giving them your vote. If the answer is yes, tell them about the reform frameworks that exist to support and protect leaders who make those commitments.

You can demand better without becoming the damage. That is what this entire book has been about.

CHAPTER 10

A Framework That Outlives Its Founders

I want to be clear about something. None of the frameworks described in this chapter were designed to be dependent on any single person. If someone picks up the values contract model and adapts it, renames it, runs with it in a direction none of us anticipated, that is not a failure. That is the point.

Frameworks are meant to travel. They are meant to be translated into different communities by different people. The American Anti-Corruption Act was designed as model legislation precisely so it could be adapted to local conditions. Ranked choice voting looks different in Alaska than it does in New York City. The BPP's 12 values are universal enough to survive translation into any community. The enforcement mechanism is specific enough to maintain accountability through it.

What matters is not who carries any of this forward. What matters is that the standards exist. That voters can point to them and say: this is what I expect from anyone who asks for my vote. That candidates can sign them and say: this is the promise I am making, and here is the mechanism that holds me to it. That when the next generation looks at how we handled this moment, they see that we did not just yell about what was broken. We built something.

The bridge is not between left and right. The bridge is between what American politics is and what it could be if we stopped accepting the unacceptable and started demanding something worthy of the people it claims to serve.

You do not need permission to cross it. Just walk.

Chapter References:
American Bar Association Task Force for American Democracy. (2025).

What we know about ranked choice voting, updated for 2025. American Bar Association.

Centola, D., Becker, J., Brackbill, D., & Baronchelli, A. (2018). Experimental evidence for tipping points in social convention. Science, 360(6393), 1116-1119.

Center for Effective Government. (2024). Democracy reform primer series. University of Chicago Harris School of Public Policy.

FairVote. (2025). Ranked choice voting. https://fairvote.org/

Gallup. (2025, October 22). Congress' job rating sinks to 15%; Trump's steady at 41%. Gallup.

National Association of Nonpartisan Reformers. (2022). Annual summit proceedings. NANR.

NBC News Data Graphics. (2025, June 25). Data shows Democratic voter registrations slipping, Republicans ticking down as independent and third-party expands. NBC News.

Potter, T., Lessig, L., et al. (2012). The American Anti-Corruption Act. RepresentUs.

RepresentUs. (2025). 2025: A year of action. Annual report.

Serrano, A. (2026, January 2). James Talarico reports raising nearly $7 million, continuing cash influx to U.S. Senate bid. The Texas Tribune.

Statista Research Department. (2025). U.S. Congress public approval rating 2025. Statista.

Talarico, J. (2025). Campaign launch remarks. September 9, 2025. Austin, Texas.

11

FOR THE CHILDREN WHO ARE WATCHING

*E*ven when we think they are not paying attention, children are studying us. They watch how we talk about the world, how we treat people who scare or anger us, and how we behave when we feel powerless. They are learning what adulthood looks like under stress.

But something has shifted. The children are no longer only watching. They are responding.

Across the United States and around the world, young people are stepping into public life with a clarity that should humble every adult who assumed the next generation was not paying attention. They are organizing walkouts, running for office, filing for ballot access, building coalitions, and confronting the very systems that many of their parents have spent years complaining about over dinner tables. Some of them are not old enough to drive. Many of them cannot yet vote. And still, they are showing up with more purpose and precision than the institutions that were supposed to protect them.

This chapter is not about turning children into activists. It is about what is already happening, right now, in real time, and what it tells us about the moment we are in.

They See the Patterns

One of the most common things young people say when asked why they stepped into civic life is some version of the same observation: the adults either cannot see what is happening, or they can see it and are choosing to do nothing about it. That is not teenage rebellion talking. That is pattern recognition.

Consider Dean Roy of Stowe, Vermont. In the summer of 2025, at the age of fourteen, Roy announced his candidacy for governor. Vermont is the only state in the country with no minimum age requirement for the office, and Roy met the sole qualification of having lived in the state for at least four years. He had lived there his entire life. The idea started as a half-joke with his eighth-grade teacher, who said that if Roy ever ran for office, he would be his campaign manager. Then Roy looked up the requirements. Then he stopped joking.

Roy spent his summer walking through his community collecting the 500 signatures needed to qualify for the ballot. He founded his own political party, the Freedom and Unity Party, because he did not see himself reflected in either major party. His platform focused on housing affordability, rising property taxes, a proposed tax on short-term rentals that are displacing long-term residents, and consolidating the state's more than one hundred school districts down to five. He challenged the sitting lieutenant governor on electric vehicle policy. He debated adults twice his age at community events. He acknowledged the irony of a fourteen-year-old running on a housing platform when he did not own a home, and then said something that landed harder than any policy brief: "When a kid in Vermont understands that there is a housing and affordability crisis, that is when you know it is bad."

Roy is not pretending he will win. He said so himself. But he also said something else: "I want to do great things for the state of Vermont. I know I am young, but I hope I can get my name out there and start building some credibility this year. That way I can run a very serious campaign when it is time." He is thinking in decades. He is fourteen.

He is not alone. In 2022, Jaylen Smith was elected mayor of Earle, Arkansas, at the age of eighteen, making him the youngest Black mayor in United States history. His priorities were not abstract. He wanted to improve public safety, address transportation, renovate abandoned housing, and tackle the food desert in his community. He won with 235 votes in a small town, but the message carried far beyond Earle. A teenager looked at the condition of his community and decided that waiting for someone older to fix it was no longer a reasonable plan.

These are not isolated stories. They are signals.

The Walkouts

In the early months of 2025, a wave of student-led walkouts swept across the United States. From East Los Angeles to Traverse City, Michigan, from Ann Arbor to the suburbs of Fort Worth, Texas, high school students left their classrooms to protest federal immigration enforcement policies. In some schools, more than half the student body walked out. At Lakeside High School in Georgia, approximately 1,500 of 2,200 students participated. Student coalitions organized a "National Shutdown" on January 30, calling on Americans to skip school and work in protest. The movement grew throughout February and continued into the spring.

These were not random outbursts. Students organized in advance. They invited media. They coordinated across schools and cities. At Ann Arbor's Community High School, student organizer Milly Sandstrom put it plainly: "Young people are the future. We have to say something now because God forbid there is a day when we cannot say what we believe and what we want to be changed." In Traverse City, sophomore Evan Kohler said: "I think it is very important to show that we care, show solidarity, and spark change in our community. This feeds into the reason we are doing this. We would like to spark change by getting more kids into politics, especially in times like these."

Some adults supported the walkouts. Some condemned them. Texas Governor Greg Abbott threatened to strip funding from schools that allowed students to leave class, and the Texas Education Agency warned that school boards could face removal for facilitating "inappropriate political activism." That response itself became a lesson for the students. In Tarrant County, Texas, senior Khai Huy Nguyen, who helped organize students at Richland High School, noted that the state's response to student speech was more telling than the walkouts themselves. Legal experts observed that First Amendment protections apply to political speech regardless of the speaker's age, and that punishing one type of demonstration more harshly than another based on its message would be unconstitutional.

Whether one agrees with the students' positions or not, the fact remains: they acted. They assessed a political situation, determined that silence was not acceptable, and organized a public response. That is civic participation. That is what democracy is supposed to produce.

CHAPTER 11

A Generation That Already Knows the Playbook

This generation did not arrive at activism out of nowhere. They inherited a trail that was blazed by young people only slightly older than themselves.

In 2018, after seventeen people were killed at Marjory Stoneman Douglas High School in Parkland, Florida, a group of surviving students did something that had never been done at that scale before. They organized the March for Our Lives, one of the largest youth-led protests in American history, drawing an estimated 200,000 to 800,000 participants to Washington, D.C., with sister marches in hundreds of cities worldwide. Students like Emma Gonzalez, David Hogg, and Cameron Kasky became household names. They were teenagers. They were told they were too young, too emotional, too naive. They helped pass the Bipartisan Safer Communities Act, the first major federal gun safety legislation in thirty years. They helped unseat forty NRA-backed candidates in the 2018 midterms. Firearms remain the leading cause of death for American children and teens, and the organization those students built is still running.

The children watching today know this history. They saw what happened when young people refused to accept that the adults in charge had it handled. They saw that grief could become strategy. They saw that anger, channeled through organization, could move legislation. And they are applying those lessons now, not just on gun violence, but across a widening range of issues where they feel the adults have either failed or stopped trying.

On November 7, 2025, a coalition of student organizations launched "Students Rise Up," coordinating walkouts and protests at hundreds of schools across the country. Their demands included free public higher education, affordable housing near campuses, job security for campus workers, safety regardless of immigration status, funding for health research and climate action, and the freedom to teach truthfully and protest without surveillance. These were not vague grievances. They were platform items, organized with the precision of a political campaign, by people still years away from their first legal vote.

A Global Mirror

What is happening in the United States is not happening in isolation. Around the world, Generation Z has emerged as one of the most consequential political forces in recent memory, and the pattern is strikingly consistent: young people who have been told their concerns do not matter are proving, through sheer collective will, that they do.

In Serbia, a student-led movement that began after a railway station canopy collapsed in Novi Sad in November 2024, killing sixteen people, grew into the largest protest movement the country had seen in decades. By March 2025, more than 300,000 people filled the streets of Belgrade. The movement, called "Students in Blockade," remained remarkably nonviolent and leaderless by design. Students marched from Belgrade to Novi Sad on foot, ninety kilometers, when the government shut down public transportation. Restaurants fed them. Universities opened their doors. The protests forced the prime minister to resign and continue to demand snap elections, transparency, and accountability. United Nations experts have called on the Serbian government to halt its crackdown. The movement is still going.

In Bangladesh in 2024, a student protest over a public-sector hiring quota system grew into a nationwide uprising that toppled the fifteen-year rule of Prime Minister Sheikh Hasina. Students formed their own political party. The movement is now widely cited as the first successful Gen Z revolution, inspiring similar uprisings in Nepal, Indonesia, the Philippines, Madagascar, Morocco, and Peru. In Nepal, young people took to the streets of Kathmandu in September 2025 after the government banned social media, demanding an end to corruption. The prime minister was replaced.

The 2025 Global Youth Participation Index found that while those under thirty are less likely to vote in elections, they are more likely to play active roles in online and in-person civic and political movements. The Carnegie Endowment's Global Protest Tracker tallied fifty-three demonstrations of 10,000 people or more across thirty-three economies in 2025 alone, the highest total since the tracker began in 2017. Many of these were youth-led. The Britannica encyclopedia, in its entry on the Gen Z protests, noted that the same generation once characterized as apathetic and disengaged had, by the end of 2025, become "one of the most unconventional and combustible political forces in recent decades."

In country after country, the story is the same. Young people who were told the system was not their concern have decided that the system is, in fact, their inheritance, and they intend to have a say in its condition before it is handed over.

What Adults Model Under Stress

This is where the chapter turns back to you.

Because the children who are stepping up are not doing so in a vacuum. They are watching how the adults around them respond to difficulty. They notice whether adults go silent or talk openly when something frightening happens. They notice whether disagreement in the house means shouting, cold distance, or careful listening. They notice whether the adults they trust seem to shrink with fear or still make room for small joys and kindness.

You do not have to present a flawless face. In fact, pretending you are never scared or confused can make the world feel even more unstable to a child, because the gap between what they sense and what you admit grows wider. A more honest model sounds like: "I am worried about what is happening, and I am still here taking care of you." Or: "I do not know exactly what will happen next, but there are things we can do and people who are working on this." Or simply: "I need a break from the news right now. Let us do something together and come back to it later."

You are teaching them that adults can feel fear and keep functioning, that concern does not have to turn into panic, and that it is possible to stay present without being consumed. The goal is not to shield them from every dark truth. It is to show them that hard truths can be faced without losing your shape.

My own daughter has been part of this awakening. I have watched her move from quietly absorbing the tension in our household to asking pointed questions about what she sees in the news, questions that are harder and more precise than anything I expected from someone her age. She is not an exception. She is representative of a generation that has been raised on information, saturated with it, and is now old enough to recognize when what they are being told does not match what they can see with their own eyes.

Courage Without Cruelty

Children pick up quickly on how we talk about "them," whoever "they" are in our current story: another party, another group, another country, people who think differently from us. If they hear only contempt, mockery, or fantasies of revenge, they learn that bravery means having enemies and enjoying their pain. If they see that courage can coexist with restraint, they learn something else: that it is possible to stand firm without becoming hard.

Courage without cruelty looks like naming harm clearly without dehumanizing the people causing it. It looks like saying "this behavior is not okay" rather than "those people are trash." It looks like explaining why certain ideas are dangerous while acknowledging that people often hold them out of fear, ignorance, or pressure, not inherent evil. It looks like letting children see you apologize when you speak too harshly, even about public figures.

None of this means being neutral. Children also need to see lines: that racism, dehumanization, and calls for violence are wrong, full stop. They need to know that you will protect them and others, not excuse cruelty in the name of "both sides." What you are modeling is that taking a stand does not require you to enjoy anyone's suffering. You are showing them a form of strength that does not depend on someone else's humiliation.

What You Leave Them With

You cannot guarantee what kind of country or world children will inherit. You can influence what they bring to it.

They will need more than fear. They will need more than slogans. They will need a sense that their feelings are valid and survivable, a model of how to disagree without destroying each other, a memory of adults who took responsibility without pretending to be invincible, and a quiet understanding that courage and kindness are not opposites.

The children who are watching now will grow up with stories about this period, some from textbooks, many from fragments of conversation, news clips, and family memories. You do not control the whole story. You do control the part where they look back and remember how you moved when things were uncertain.

But here is the part that this chapter must now account for: some of those children are not waiting for the story to be written about them. They are writing it themselves. A fourteen-year-old in Vermont is collecting signatures for a gubernatorial campaign because he believes his state deserves better. An eighteen-year-old in Arkansas is governing a town because no one else stepped up. Thousands of high school students across the country are walking out of class because they have decided that silence is complicity. Hundreds of thousands of young people in Serbia are marching ninety kilometers on foot because their government will not listen any other way.

If all you can manage on some days is to be a little more honest, a little less cruel, and a little more consistent in your small promises, that is not nothing. That is a child's first lesson in what it means to live among others without giving up on yourself.

But do not be surprised if they do more than watch. Do not be surprised if they lead.

They are already leading. The only question left is whether we are brave enough to follow.

Chapter References:

Amnesty International. (2025, October 17). The Gen-Z movement: This is why we are risking our lives to protest. https://www.amnesty.org/en/latest/campaigns/2025/10/the-gen-z-movement-this-is-why-were-risking-our-lives-to-protest/

Bilow, P. (2025, July 17). Stowe teen trains for a different race. Stowe Reporter / VTDigger. https://vtdigger.org/2025/07/20/stowe-teen-preps-for-gubernatorial-race/

Britannica. (2025, November 20). Generation Z protests. https://www.britannica.com/event/Generation-Z-protests

Carnegie Endowment for International Peace. (2025, December). Corruption, overreach, and hardship: The global drivers of protests in 2025. https://carnegieendowment.org/emissary/2025/12/global-protests-2025-genz-corruption-economy

CBS News Detroit. (2026, February 5). Hundreds of Ann Arbor high school students walk out in protest of latest ICE activities. https://www.cbsnews.com/detroit/news/ann-arbor-high-school-students-walk-out-ice-operations/

CHAPTER 11

Council on Foreign Relations. (2025, November 20). How global Gen Z protests have shocked and transformed governments. https://www.cfr.org/articles/how-global-gen-z-protests-have-shocked-and-transformed-governments

European Democracy Hub. (2025, December 8). Misunderstanding youth activism: How young people are rewriting democracy. https://europeandemocracyhub.epd.eu/misunderstanding-youth-activism/

Fort Worth Report. (2026, February 5). Student walkouts prompt warning from Texas leaders, raising First Amendment concerns. https://fortworthreport.org/2026/02/05/student-walkouts-prompt-warning-from-texas-leaders-raising-first-amendment-concerns/

Free Press Journal. (2025, November 28). Who is Dean Roy? The 14-year-old from Vermont in the New England region running for governor. https://www.freepressjournal.in/education/who-is-dean-roy-the-14-year-old-from-vermont-in-the-new-england-region-running-for-governor

Journal of Democracy. (2025). How Serbian students created the largest protest movement in decades. https://www.journalofdemocracy.org/online-exclusive/how-serbian-students-created-the-largest-protest-movement-in-decades/

March For Our Lives. (2025). About us. https://marchforourlives.org/about-us/

NEWS10. (2025, December 28). Meet the 14-year-old vying for governor of Vermont. https://www.news10.com/news/meet-the-14-year-old-vying-for-governor-of-vermont/

OHCHR. (2025, August). Serbia must halt crackdown on student movement, uphold human rights and academic freedom: UN experts. https://www.ohchr.org/en/press-releases/2025/08/serbia-must-halt-crackdown-student-movement-uphold-human-rights-and-academic

Open Government Partnership. (2025, September 16). The youth participation crisis. https://www.opengovpartnership.org/stories/the-youth-participation-crisis/

PEOPLE / Yahoo News. (2025, December 10). 14-year-old hopes to be Vermont's next governor after forming his own party to get on the ballot. https://www.yahoo.com/news/articles/14-old-hopes-vermonts-next-173330050.html

Platform for Peace and Humanity. (2025, December 17). Serbia's historic student-led protest movement (2024-2025). https://peacehumanity.org/monitor/serbias-historic-student-led-protest-movement-2024-2025/

School of International Service, American University. (2025, November 6). Why do students lead protest movements? https://www.american.edu/sis/news/20251106-why-do-students-lead-protest-movements.cfm

Students Rise Up. (2025). https://www.studentsriseup.org/

The Patriot Post, Birmingham Community Charter High School. (2025). 2025 high school student walkouts across the San Fernando Valley. https://bcchspatriotpost.com/25233/uncategorized/2025-high-school-student-walkouts-across-the-san-fernando-valley/

The Ticker. (2026, February). From protest walkouts to Turning Point launch, students get engaged politically. https://www.traverseticker.com/news/from-protest-walkouts-to-turning-point-launch-students-get-engaged-politically/

Wikipedia contributors. (2026). Gen Z protests. Wikipedia. https://en.wikipedia.org/wiki/Gen_Z_protests

Wikipedia contributors. (2026). Jaylen Smith (politician). Wikipedia. https://en.wikipedia.org/wiki/Jaylen_Smith_(politician)

Wikipedia contributors. (2026). March for Our Lives. Wikipedia. https://en.wikipedia.org/wiki/March_for_Our_Lives

12

IF YOU DO NOTHING ELSE

By now you have seen more than enough to feel overwhelmed. There are phases and tactics and roles and risks. You may be wondering what any of it adds up to in your own life, especially if you cannot imagine joining a movement, changing your job, or rearranging your days.

This chapter is for that moment.

It is not a summary of the book. It is not a test of commitment. It is a small, deliberate list of things that matter even if you never do anything that looks like activism from the outside.

This chapter exists because most lives remain ordinary even in extraordinary times. That is not a failure. It is the human condition. History does not only turn on heroes or public figures. It rests on millions of people who quietly decide what they will and will not become, often without recognition and often without certainty.

If you do nothing else, let this chapter meet you where you are.

A Short List of Non-Negotiables

If you do nothing else, consider holding to a few non-negotiables. These are lines you decide in advance not to cross, even when you are tired, scared, or pressured.

For example:

I will not celebrate cruelty. I may get angry. I may want accountability. But I will not enjoy other people's suffering, even when they are on the "other side."

I will not knowingly spread lies. If I learn something I shared was false or misleading, I will correct it instead of doubling down.

I will not dehumanize entire groups. I can criticize behavior, policies, and systems without treating any category of people as less than human.

I will not look away from obvious injustice in my immediate reach. I may not fix it, but I will not pretend it is fine.

Your list may look different. The point is not to borrow someone else's values, but to choose a handful of commitments that feel serious and sustainable *for you*.

Non-negotiables are not about being perfect. They are about knowing, in advance, who you refuse to become. When those lines are clear in your own mind, you are less likely to drift past them by accident.

Acting Imperfectly but Deliberately

Waiting until you have the perfect plan is one of the most reliable ways to do nothing.

If you do nothing else, practice making small, deliberate choices instead of waiting for flawless clarity:

Support one trustworthy institution, outlet, or group with a modest, regular contribution.

Stay in one difficult conversation a little longer than you otherwise would, but leave before it becomes destructive.

Volunteer for one task that supports others, even if it is unglamorous and invisible.

Take one regular break from the news to do something that restores you, so that when you return, you are capable of more than doom-scrolling.

You will misjudge things. You will sometimes act too quickly or too late. You will sometimes say the wrong thing. That is not a reason to stop. It is a reason to adjust and continue.

There is a quiet lie that circulates in moments like this: that only loud, visible, or sacrificial lives count. That if your days remain focused on work, family, health, or survival, you are somehow failing the moment.

That is not true.

Deliberate imperfection is better than spotless paralysis. Ordinary consistency matters more than dramatic intention.

Choosing Dignity Over Despair

Despair is not only a feeling. It is a story:

"Nothing I do matters, and nothing anyone does changes anything."

That story can feel comforting in a twisted way because it absolves you from choosing. If nothing matters, you are off the hook.

Dignity tells a different story:

"I may not control the outcome, but I control what I contribute."

"I am responsible for the harm I do, not for solving everything."

"My worth is not measured by victories, but by whether I stayed in honest relationship with what I believed was right."

Responsibility is not the same thing as guilt. You are accountable for what you choose to do and not do within your reach, not for the entire trajectory of history. Carrying guilt for outcomes you cannot control does not make you more ethical. It only makes you more exhausted.

If you do nothing else, refuse to let despair be your final author. You can feel it, name it, even sit with it. But you do not have to live by it.

Sometimes dignity looks like visible courage. Sometimes it looks like quiet refusal: not laughing at the cruel joke, not joining the pile-on, not signing the paper that harms someone else. These moments are small, but they are where your life is actually lived.

Leaving the Door Open

There may be periods when all of this feels far away. You might need to pull back to care for a child, a parent, your health, or your mind. You might move, change jobs, or simply shut down for a while.

If you do nothing else, leave the door open for yourself and for others.

Do not burn the bridge to every space where people are trying, even if you cannot be in those spaces right now.

CHAPTER 12

Do not declare that you will never care again, never risk again, never speak again.

Do not close your heart so completely that, when circumstances change, you cannot return.

Leaving the door open means staying willing to re-enter the story later, in whatever way makes sense then. It also means staying willing to welcome others back without demanding explanations or purity tests.

Most of these choices will not feel political when you are making them. They will feel personal. Relational. Ordinary. They will happen in conversations, workplaces, classrooms, kitchens, and quiet moments when no one is watching.

That is where they matter most.

You do not have to know what your role will be in five years. You do not have to commit to a lifetime of effort. You only have to avoid slamming the door on the possibility that you, and the people around you, can grow into more honest and courageous versions of yourselves.

If you do nothing else with this book, let it nudge you toward a small set of lines you will hold, a handful of imperfect actions you will take on purpose, a stubborn sense of your own dignity, and an open door.

That may not look like much from the outside.

From the inside, it is the difference between drifting and living.

APPENDIX A: ALIGNING YOUR STRENGTHS WITH WHAT YOU CAN DO RIGHT NOW

Things You Can Do Right Now

Writing & Synthesis

- You think clearly on the page, connect ideas, explain complex things, or tell stories that help others make sense of events.
- Write essays, letters, newsletters, or books. Document what is happening. Translate complex issues into plain language. Write for local outlets or community groups. Keep a public or private record that others may need later.

Speaking & Storytelling

- You are comfortable talking, explaining, or being visible. People listen to you or feel understood when you speak.
- Create short videos or podcasts. Speak at community events. Talk to family, coworkers, or faith groups. Serve as

a spokesperson when others prefer not to. Normalize calm, clear speech under pressure.

Research & Pattern Recognition

- You notice inconsistencies, trends, and long-term patterns. You like evidence, timelines, and details.
- Track policy changes, appointments, and court rulings. Create timelines or explainers. Support journalists and watchdog groups with research. Preserve documentation others might overlook.

Organizing & Logistics

- You are good at planning, coordinating, scheduling, and making things actually happen.
- Organize meetings, rides, childcare, food, or supplies. Help protests or events run smoothly. Coordinate volunteers. Handle behind-the-scenes work that keeps others effective.

Relationship Building & Bridging

- You connect people across differences and notice who feels isolated or burned out.
- Build coalitions. Host small gatherings. Introduce people doing similar work. Keep conversations open across political or cultural divides. Reduce fragmentation.

Caregiving & Emotional Support

- You are steady, empathetic, and good at supporting people under stress.
- Offer emotional support to activists, students, or vulnerable people. Create spaces for rest and reflection.

APPENDIX A: ALIGNING YOUR STRENGTHS WITH WHAT YOU CAN...

Check in on those targeted or burned out. Help people stay human in hard moments.

Visibility & Risk Tolerance

- You can handle attention, criticism, or pressure without collapsing.
- Take on public-facing roles. Speak to media. Be present at protests or hearings. Absorb visibility so others don't have to. Model calm courage.

Detail-Oriented & Procedural Thinking

- You understand systems, rules, and how institutions actually function.
- Monitor elections, budgets, and administrative changes. Volunteer as a poll worker or observer. Explain how laws or rules affect everyday life. Catch quiet erosion early.

Artistic & Creative Expression

- You communicate through art, humor, music, design, or symbolism.
- Create visual art, performances, or satire that deflates fear and reaches people emotionally. Make the movement human and accessible.

Ethics, Teaching & Mentorship

- You naturally help others think through values, history, and moral implications.
- Teach classes, lead discussion groups, mentor younger people. Help others understand why norms matter and how to think critically without panic.

Protection & De-Escalation

- You think about safety, boundaries, and reducing harm.
- Serve as a safety marshal or legal observer. Help de-escalate conflict. Plan for accessibility and risk reduction. Protect people rather than escalating confrontation.

Quiet Consistency

- You may not want visibility, but you show up reliably and follow through.
- Support one or two efforts long-term. Vote consistently. Donate modestly. Model integrity at work and home. Hold your non-negotiables even when no one is watching.

APPENDIX B: HIGH-LEVEL STRATEGIC MOVES TO BLOCK AUTHORITARIAN PLAYBOOK TACTICS

What This Looks Like in Practice
Why It Works

Permanent crisis narrative

- Normalize calm, long-term framing
- Host forums, teach-ins, or town halls focused on evidence and timelines rather than outrage. Correct exaggerated "emergency" claims in plain language.
- Crisis fatigue weakens consent. Calm reframing denies emotional escalation and preserves public trust.

Divide and conquer society

- Build broad, cross-identity coalitions
- Unite labor, faith groups, veterans, students, professionals, and local leaders around minimal shared goals like rule of law and fair elections.

- Authoritarian systems fail when opposition refuses to fracture into silos.

Use democratic language to hollow democracy

- Translate abstraction into consequences
- Explain what laws *actually* do in daily life. Create checklists of democratic norms and show which ones are being eroded.
- People resist more effectively when they understand tangible impacts.

Rig elections while keeping rituals

- Flood the process with legitimacy
- Recruit poll workers, observers, and voter-registration organizers. Document irregularities in real time. Support court challenges.
- Rigging relies on low visibility and low participation.

Capture one party completely

- Strategic party infiltration
- Encourage values-aligned candidates to run as Republicans in red districts. Register and vote in primaries where rules allow.
- Shifts outcomes without needing to "flip" districts ideologically.

Personalize power around one leader

- Decentralize leadership deliberately

- Avoid single charismatic leaders. Rotate spokespeople. Build parallel local leadership structures.
- Makes movements harder to decapitate or co-opt.

Erode trust in independent media

- Build parallel credibility networks
- Support investigative journalism, local outlets, and community newsletters. Share corrections loudly.
- Truth survives when trusted locally, not centrally imposed.

Weaponize fear and punitive culture

- Visible, disciplined nonviolence
- Organize peaceful protests with clear conduct norms, marshals, and de-escalation teams.
- Denies justification for repression and attracts broader support.

Undermine courts and rule of law

- Public defense of institutions
- Organize petitions, protests, and professional statements defending judicial independence. Support litigation groups.
- Raises political cost of institutional capture.

Co-opt watchdog agencies

- Build civilian oversight substitutes
- Support NGOs, data journalists, citizen monitoring groups, and whistleblower protection networks.

- Keeps accountability alive even when institutions are compromised.

Monopolize force and intimidate selectively

- Protect and document targets
- Create legal defense funds, rapid response networks, and documentation teams.
- Repression weakens when costs are immediate and visible.

Digital authoritarianism and disinformation

- Harden movement infrastructure
- Use secure communication, backup channels, offline networks, and coordinated fact-checking brigades.
- Prevents silencing through throttling or harassment.

Rewrite history and control education

- Parallel education systems
- Support independent educators, museums, podcasts, and community learning spaces.
- Preserves memory when official narratives are distorted.

Create elite buy-in through patronage

- Expose and isolate patronage networks
- Track contracts, conflicts of interest, and loyalty appointments. Apply public pressure to businesses and donors.
- Corruption loses power when exposed repeatedly and clearly.

Force false binary choices

- Maintain a "bridge" posture
- Refuse extremes. Keep coalitions wide. Allow disagreement without rupture.
- Blocks polarization, which authoritarians require to govern.

APPENDIX C: GO DEEPER

RECOMMENDED READINGS

The following works shaped the thinking behind this book. Each explores patterns of democratic erosion, propaganda, political psychology, and institutional drift to deepen your knowledge.

DEMOCRATIC EROSION & INSTITUTIONAL DRIFT

How Democracies Die (Crown, 2018)

Authors: Steven Levitsky and Daniel Ziblatt

About the Book: A comparative study of how democracies decline gradually through institutional erosion rather than sudden coups.

Connection to This Work: This book provides the structural backbone for understanding how normalization, partisan loyalty, and weakened guardrails allow democratic systems to unravel quietly over time.

On Tyranny (Tim Duggan Books, 2017)

Author: Timothy Snyder

About the Book: A concise set of historical lessons drawn from twentieth century authoritarian regimes.

Connection to This Work: Snyder's framework reinforces the idea that early warning signs matter and that civic responsibility begins before collapse becomes obvious.

Twilight of Democracy (Doubleday, 2020)

Author: Anne Applebaum

About the Book: An examination of why intellectual and political elites drift toward illiberalism.

Connection to This Work: Applebaum helps illuminate how ideological shifts among elites accelerate broader democratic backsliding.

Propaganda & Media Systems

Manufacturing Consent (Pantheon Books, 1988)

Authors: Edward S. Herman and Noam Chomsky

About the Book: A foundational analysis of how media institutions filter information through systemic incentives.

Connection to This Work: It offers a structural explanation for how narratives are shaped long before they reach the public.

Network Propaganda (Oxford University Press, 2018)

Authors: Yochai Benkler, Robert Faris, and Hal Roberts

About the Book: A data driven study of misinformation and asymmetric media ecosystems in the digital age.

Connection to This Work: This research clarifies how online networks amplify polarization and distort democratic discourse.

Amusing Ourselves to Death (Viking Penguin, 1985)

Author: Neil Postman

About the Book: A critique of how entertainment culture reshapes public conversation and political seriousness.

Connection to This Work: Postman's warning about spectacle over substance helps explain the emotional volatility of modern political life.

POLITICAL PSYCHOLOGY & GROUP DYNAMICS

The Righteous Mind (Pantheon Books, 2012)

Author: Jonathan Haidt

About the Book: An exploration of moral foundations theory and why political opponents see the world so differently.

Connection to This Work: Haidt's research helps decode the emotional drivers beneath ideological conflict.

The True Believer (Harper & Brothers, 1951)

Author: Eric Hoffer

About the Book: A classic study of mass movements and the psychology of ideological commitment.

Connection to This Work: Hoffer's insights illuminate why individuals are drawn to rigid belief systems during unstable periods.

Historical Foundations

The Origins of Totalitarianism (Harcourt, Brace & Co., 1951)

Author: Hannah Arendt

About the Book: A foundational analysis of totalitarian systems and their structural mechanics.

Connection to This Work: Arendt provides the long view that informs the pattern recognition at the heart of this book.

Strongmen (W. W. Norton & Company, 2020)

Author: Ruth Ben Ghiat

About the Book: A comparative study of modern authoritarian leaders and the tactics they share.

Connection to This Work: This text reinforces the recurring strategies that transcend geography and political branding.

The United States Constitution (1787)

About the Document: The foundational legal framework of the United States government.

Connection to This Work: Understanding the original structure clarifies what is at stake when institutional norms erode.

COURAGE

APPENDIX C: GO DEEPER

We Can Do Hard Things (Dial Press, 2022)

Author: Glennon Doyle

About the Book: A reflective exploration of emotional resilience, vulnerability, and the practice of telling the truth in uncomfortable moments.

Connection to This Work: This book affirms the courage required to remain present with difficult emotions, a necessary precursor to confronting the larger social and civic realities examined in this work.

Dare to Lead (Random House, 2018)

Author: Brené Brown

About the Book: An examination of leadership grounded in vulnerability, accountability, and the willingness to engage in difficult conversations.

Connection to This Work: This book reinforces courage as a practiced discipline, one that requires truth-telling and emotional risk within systems that often reward silence and conformity.

ABOUT THE AUTHOR

Justin C. Ryan writes at the intersection of lived experience, institutional systems, and human vulnerability. His work is shaped by more than a decade of service in the United States Air Force, followed by senior leadership roles in cyber risk management, governance, and sensitive data stewardship within global financial institutions.

In the military, he learned discipline, hierarchy, and the mechanics of command. He saw how mission clarity can unify people and how institutional language can both protect and conceal. After leaving the Air Force, he moved into the private sector, working within complex global organizations where risk is modeled, measured, mitigated, and sometimes quietly transferred. There he developed a deep understanding of how power distributes itself through policy, compliance frameworks, incentive structures, and information systems.

Across those environments, Justin observed something consistent. Institutions rarely fail all at once. They adapt. They normalize. They protect their own narratives. Accountability becomes procedural rather than moral. Language becomes technical rather than truthful. Over time, individuals inside those systems can begin to doubt their own perceptions, not because they are naïve, but because the system itself reshapes what feels acceptable.

Those observations inform his writing.

Justin approaches politics not as a partisan commentator but as a systems thinker. He is interested in how structures drift, how narratives are engineered, how incentives distort behavior, and how ordinary citizens slowly acclimate to changes they once would have resisted. His background in cybersecurity and governance sharpened his ability to recognize patterns, vulnerabilities, and cascading risk. That same lens is applied in Are You Mad Yet? to examine democratic erosion, media manipulation, and institutional fragility.

At the same time, his work is grounded in empathy. He believes dehumanization is one of the earliest warning signs of institutional decay. He refuses to reduce people to caricatures, even those whose political positions he strongly opposes. For Justin, clarity does not require cruelty. Moral courage does not require humiliation.

Writing became the place where his professional insights and personal reflections converged. It is where technical observation meets human consequence. Where policy becomes lived experience. Where systems thinking reconnects to individual agency.

Are You Mad Yet? is not written from above or from the sidelines. It is written from within the confusion of this moment, by someone who has worked inside large institutions and understands both their necessity and their fragility. It is the work of a citizen who believes that awareness is not panic, that anger can be diagnostic rather than destructive, and that responsibility begins with perception.

Justin lives between Bangkok, Thailand and San Antonio, Texas, navigating cultures, political climates, and identities that do not always align neatly. He is the father of three children who continually challenge him to think more honestly and love more bravely. In his free time, he paints, drawn to color and form as another way of making sense of complexity.

He writes because clarity matters. And because looking away is a choice.

                        instagram.com/Justinryanart
                        tiktok.com/@bridgepartypact

Made in the USA
Coppell, TX
01 March 2026

72544794R00105